IN ASSOCIATION WITH
SQA

HODDER GIBSON

Model Papers

WITH ANSWERS

PLUS: Official SQA 2014 & 2015 Past Papers With Answers

National 5
Spanish

Model Papers, 2014 & 2015 Exams

D1460279

HODDER GIBSON
AN HACHETTE UK COMPANY

This book contains the official SQA and 2015 Exams for National 5 Spanish, with associated SQA approved answers modified from the official marking instructions that accompany the paper.

In addition the book contains model papers, together with answers, plus study skills advice. These papers, some of which may include a ' limited number of previously published SQA questions, have been specially commissioned by Hodder Gibson, and have been written by experienced senior teachers and examiners in line with the new National 5 syllabus and assessment outlines, Spring 2013. This is not SQA material but has been devised to provide further practice for National 5 examinations in 2014 and beyond.

Hodder Gibson is grateful to the copyright holders, as credited on the final page of the Answer Section, for permission to use their material. Every effort has been made to trace the copyright holders and to obtain their permission for the use of copyright material. Hodder Gibson will be happy to receive information allowing us to rectify any error or omission in future editions.

Hachette UK's policy is to use papers that are natural, renewable and recyclable products and made from wood grown in sustainable forests. The logging and manufacturing processes are expected to conform to the environmental regulations of the country of origin.

Orders: please contact Bookpoint Ltd, 130 Park Drive, Milton Park, Abingdon, Oxon OX14 4SE. Telephone: (44) 01235 827720. Fax: (44) 01235 400454. Lines are open 9.00–5.00, Monday to Saturday, with a 24-hour message answering service. Visit our website at www.hoddereducation.co.uk. Hodder Gibson can be contacted direct on: Tel: 0141 848 1609; Fax: 0141 889 6315; email: hoddergibson@hodder.co.uk

This collection first published in 2015 by
Hodder Gibson, an imprint of Hodder Education,
An Hachette UK Company
2a Christie Street
Paisley PA1 1NB

Typeset by Aptara, Inc.

Printed in the UK

A catalogue record for this title is available from the British Library

ISBN: 978-1-4718-6067-6

3 2 1

2016 2015

Introduction

Study Skills – what you need to know to pass exams!

Pause for thought

Many students might skip quickly through a page like this. After all, we all know how to revise. Do you really though?

Think about this:

"IF YOU ALWAYS DO WHAT YOU ALWAYS DO, YOU WILL ALWAYS GET WHAT YOU HAVE ALWAYS GOT."

Do you like the grades you get? Do you want to do better? If you get full marks in your assessment, then that's great! Change nothing! This section is just to help you get that little bit better than you already are.

There are two main parts to the advice on offer here. The first part highlights fairly obvious things but which are also very important. The second part makes suggestions about revision that you might not have thought about but which WILL help you.

Part 1

DOH! It's so obvious but …

Start revising in good time

Don't leave it until the last minute – this will make you panic.

Make a revision timetable that sets out work time AND play time.

Sleep and eat!

Obvious really, and very helpful. Avoid arguments or stressful things too – even games that wind you up. You need to be fit, awake and focused!

Know your place!

Make sure you know exactly **WHEN and WHERE** your exams are.

Know your enemy!

Make sure you know what to expect in the exam.

How is the paper structured?

How much time is there for each question?

What types of question are involved?

Which topics seem to come up time and time again?

Which topics are your strongest and which are your weakest?

Are all topics compulsory or are there choices?

Learn by DOING!

There is no substitute for past papers and practice papers – they are simply essential! Tackling this collection of papers and answers is exactly the right thing to be doing as your exams approach.

Part 2

People learn in different ways. Some like low light, some bright. Some like early morning, some like evening / night. Some prefer warm, some prefer cold. But everyone uses their BRAIN and the brain works when it is active. Passive learning – sitting gazing at notes – is the most INEFFICIENT way to learn anything. Below you will find tips and ideas for making your revision more effective and maybe even more enjoyable. What follows gets your brain active, and active learning works!

Activity 1 – Stop and review

Step 1

When you have done no more than 5 minutes of revision reading STOP!

Step 2

Write a heading in your own words which sums up the topic you have been revising.

Step 3

Write a summary of what you have revised in no more than two sentences. Don't fool yourself by saying, "I know it, but I cannot put it into words". That just means you don't know it well enough. If you cannot write your summary, revise that section again, knowing that you must write a summary at the end of it. Many of you will have notebooks full of blue/black ink writing. Many of the pages will not be especially attractive or memorable so try to liven them up a bit with colour as you are reviewing and rewriting. **This is a great memory aid, and memory is the most important thing.**

Activity 2 – Use technology!

Why should everything be written down? Have you thought about "mental" maps, diagrams, cartoons and colour to help you learn? And rather than write down notes, why not record your revision material?

What about having a text message revision session with friends? Keep in touch with them to find out how and what they are revising and share ideas and questions.

Why not make a video diary where you tell the camera what you are doing, what you think you have learned and what you still have to do? No one has to see or hear it, but the process of having to organise your thoughts in a formal way to explain something is a very important learning practice.

Be sure to make use of electronic files. You could begin to summarise your class notes. Your typing might be slow, but it will get faster and the typed notes will be easier to read than the scribbles in your class notes. Try to add different fonts and colours to make your work stand out. You can easily Google relevant pictures, cartoons and diagrams which you can copy and paste to make your work more attractive and **MEMORABLE**.

Activity 3 – This is it. Do this and you will know lots!

Step 1

In this task you must be very honest with yourself! Find the SQA syllabus for your subject (www.sqa.org.uk). Look at how it is broken down into main topics called MANDATORY knowledge. That means stuff you MUST know.

Step 2

BEFORE you do ANY revision on this topic, write a list of everything that you already know about the subject. It might be quite a long list but you only need to write it once. It shows you all the information that is already in your long-term memory so you know what parts you do not need to revise!

Step 3

Pick a chapter or section from your book or revision notes. Choose a fairly large section or a whole chapter to get the most out of this activity.

With a buddy, use Skype, Facetime, Twitter or any other communication you have, to play the game "If this is the answer, what is the question?". For example, if you are revising Geography and the answer you provide is "meander", your buddy would have to make up a question like "What is the word that describes a feature of a river where it flows slowly and bends often from side to side?".

Make up 10 "answers" based on the content of the chapter or section you are using. Give this to your buddy to solve while you solve theirs.

Step 4

Construct a wordsearch of at least 10 × 10 squares. You can make it as big as you like but keep it realistic. Work together with a group of friends. Many apps allow you to make wordsearch puzzles online. The words and phrases can go in any direction and phrases can be split. Your puzzle must only contain facts linked to the topic you are revising. Your task is to find 10 bits of information to hide in your puzzle, but you must not repeat information that you used in Step 3. DO NOT show where the words are. Fill up empty squares with random letters. Remember to keep a note of where your answers are hidden but do not show your friends. When you have a complete puzzle, exchange it with a friend to solve each other's puzzle.

Step 5

Now make up 10 questions (not "answers" this time) based on the same chapter used in the previous two tasks. Again, you must find NEW information that you have not yet used. Now it's getting hard to find that new information! Again, give your questions to a friend to answer.

Step 6

As you have been doing the puzzles, your brain has been actively searching for new information. Now write a NEW LIST that contains only the new information you have discovered when doing the puzzles. Your new list is the one to look at repeatedly for short bursts over the next few days. Try to remember more and more of it without looking at it. After a few days, you should be able to add words from your second list to your first list as you increase the information in your long-term memory.

FINALLY! Be inspired...

Make a list of different revision ideas and beside each one write **THINGS I HAVE** tried, **THINGS I WILL** try and **THINGS I MIGHT** try. Don't be scared of trying something new.

And remember – "FAIL TO PREPARE AND PREPARE TO FAIL!"

National 5 Spanish

The course

The National 5 Spanish course aims to enable you to develop the ability to read, listen, talk and write in Spanish, that is to understand and use Spanish, and to apply your knowledge and understanding of the language. The course offers the opportunity to develop detailed language skills in the real-life contexts of society, learning, employability, and culture.

How the course is graded

The course assessment will take the form of a performance and a written exam.

- The performance will be a presentation and discussion with your teacher, which will be recorded and marked by your teacher.
- The written exam will take place in May and this book will help you practise for it.

The exams

Reading and Writing

- Exam time: 1 hour 30 minutes
- Total marks: 50
- Weighting in final grade: 50%

What you have to do

- Read three passages of just under 200 words each, and answer questions about them in English.
- Write 120–150 words in Spanish in the form of an email, applying for a job or work placement: there will be six bullet points for you to address.

Listening

- Exam time: 25 minutes
- Total marks: 20
- Weighting in final grade: 20%

What you have to do

- Part 1: listen to a presentation in Spanish, and answer questions in English.
- Part 2: listen to a conversation in Spanish, and answer questions about it in English.

How to improve your mark!

Every year, examiners notice the same kind of mistakes being made, and they also regularly come across some excellent work. They give advice in the three key areas of reading, listening and writing to help students do better. Here are some key points from their advice.

Reading

Make sure that your Reading answers include detail. Use each question as a guide to where to look, and what to look for. In the question there will be a clear guide to the context for the answer. Detailed answers are generally required, so pay particular attention to words like "más", "siempre", "bastante", etc. and to negatives. "Los sábados por la tarde" isn't just Saturday, and "a principios del mes de agosto" isn't just August, so be prepared to give all the details you can find.

Make sure you get the details of numbers, days, times etc. right.

Take care when using a dictionary when a word has more than one meaning. Learn to choose the correct meaning from a list of meanings in the dictionary.

Beware of false friends: "compartir" means share, not compare, and "esta de buen humor" does not mean he has a sense of humour, rather he is in a good mood.

In responding to the questions in the Reading papers, you should be guided by the number of points awarded for each question. You should give as much detail in your answer as you have understood, but you should not put down everything which is in the original text, as you would be wasting time. The question itself usually indicates the amount of information required by stating in bold, e.g. "**Mention 2 of them**". Often there are more than two possibilities, but choose the two you are happiest with and stick to them. Watch out for questions where two details are required for one mark. When you must give two details for the one mark, it will be highlighted in bold in the question.

Note that there will be a question in one of the reading papers which asks about the overall purpose of the writing. This will always be a "supported" question such as a box to tick or a true/false choice.

You should re-read your answers to make sure that they make sense and that your English expression is as good as it can be.

Listening

This is the paper that improves most with practice. So use the listening papers in this book several times to get used to the format of the exam.

Not giving enough detail is still a major reason for candidates losing marks. Many answers are correct as far as they go, but are not sufficiently detailed to score marks. The rules for Reading also apply here.

You hear each of the Listening texts three times, so make use of the third listening to check the accuracy and specific details of your answers.

Be sure you are able to give accurate answers through confident knowledge of numbers, common adjectives, weather expressions, prepositions and question words, so that some of the "easier" points of information are not lost through lack of sufficiently accurate details.

In responding to the questions in the Listening papers, you should be guided by the number of points awarded for each question, and by the wording of the question. You should give as much detail in your answer as you have understood, but you should not write down everything you hear. The question itself usually indicates the amount of information required by stating in bold, e.g. "**Mention 2 of them**".

Make sure you put a line through any notes you have made.

Writing

This, along with Talking, is often where students do best. However, frequently, the language used by candidates tackling Writing dips to a basic level and leads to pieces not being truly developed. Make sure you have some good material prepared and learned, ready to use in the exam.

Also, where learners write pieces that are too lengthy, this certainly does not help their performance. So stick to 20–30 words per bullet point.

On the whole, the majority of candidates write well, and the range of language used is impressive. So look at the success criteria in the answer section and try to model your Writing on it. This applies particularly to the last two bullet points.

You should ensure that you are careful when you read the information regarding the job you are applying for, and make sure your answer is tailored to fit that. Depending on the job, you may have to alter your strengths or the experience you are claiming. Use your dictionary to make sure you know what the job actually is, if necessary.

Use the dictionary to check the accuracy of what you have written (spelling, accents, genders etc.) but not to create new sentences, particularly when dealing with the last two bullet points. You should have everything you need prepared when you come into the exam.

Be aware of the extended criteria to be used in assessing performances in Writing, so that you know what is required in terms of content, accuracy, range and variety of language to achieve the "good" and "very good" categories. Ensure that your handwriting is legible (particularly when writing in Spanish) and distinguish clearly between rough notes and what you wish to be considered as final answers. Make sure you score out your notes!

You should bear the following points in mind:

- There are six bullet points to answer: the first four are always the same, the last two vary from year to year.
- Each of the first four bullet points should have between 20 and 30 words to address it properly.
- To get a mark of satisfactory or above, you must address the last two bullet points properly.
- You will need to have at least 15–20 words for each of these last two points, but do not try to write too much for these.
- You will be assessed on how well you have answered the points, and on the accuracy of your language.
- For a mark of "good" or "very good", you should have some complex language, such as longer, varied sentences and conjunctions.

Good luck!

Remember that the rewards for passing National 5 Spanish are well worth it! Your pass will help you get the future you want for yourself. In the exam, be confident in your own ability. If you're not sure how to answer a question, trust your instincts and give it a go anyway – keep calm and don't panic! GOOD LUCK!

Model Paper 1

Whilst this Model Paper has been specially commissioned by Hodder Gibson for use as practice for the National 5 exams, the key reference documents remain the SQA Specimen Paper 2013 and the SQA Past Papers 2014 and 2015.

National Qualifications
MODEL PAPER 1

Spanish Reading

Duration — 1 hour and 30 minutes

Total marks — 30

READING — 30 marks

Read all THREE texts and attempt ALL questions.

Write your answers clearly, in **English**, in the spaces provided in this booklet.

You may use a Spanish dictionary.

Additional space for answers is provided at the end of this booklet. If you use this space you must clearly identify the question number you are attempting.

Use **blue** or **black** ink.

There is a separate question and answer booklet for Writing. You must complete your answer for Writing in the question and answer booklet for Writing.

Before leaving the examination room you must give both booklets to the Invigilator; if you do not, you may lose all the marks for this paper.

HODDER GIBSON
LEARN MORE

MARKS

READING — 30 marks

Text 1

You read this article, aimed at people who wish to eat healthily, but lose weight as well.

Guía para comer sano

Como regla general, debes escoger alimentos que sean bajos en grasas saturadas y en colesterol. También debes limitar tu ingesta de azúcar y sal. Debes comer más alimentos con fibra, como frutas, vegetales y cereales.

Si quieres perder algunos kilos, piensa en la regla número 1: ¡no dejes de comer ni se te ocurra hacer dieta! Eso sí, si quieres mantener tu peso, no puedes comer todo lo que quieras sin control. A continuación, unos pequeños consejos para que no comas más de lo que debes.

Come todas las frutas y verduras que quieres. Bebe mucha agua. El agua es un nutriente esencial. No esperes a tener sed para beber. Desayuna ... y bien. El desayuno es la comida más importante del día y te mantendrá llena de energía todo el día. Si no lo haces, estarás todo el día con hambre y comerás de más.

Cena ligero optando por las carnes blancas y magras o el pescado. Evita siempre que puedas las comidas muy saladas, las salsas, los fritos y las golosinas. De postre: yogur desnatado o fruta aunque un helado fresquito es ideal para ayudarte a hacer la digestión. Come cinco veces al día. Es mejor para el estómago y para el cerebro, y evitará que piques entre horas.

Questions

(a) The opening paragraph gives three pieces of advice: give any **two** of them.   **2**

_____

_____

(b) According to the article what is rule number one for those wishing to lose weight?   **1**

_____

(c) What advice is given about drinking water? Mention **one** thing.   **1**

_____

(d) What will happen if you don't eat a good breakfast? Mention **two** things.   **2**

_____

_____

MARKS | DO NOT WRITE IN THIS MARGIN

Text 1 Questions (continued)

(e) You are given advice on what kind of food to avoid. Tick (✓) the correct boxes.   **2**

Big salads	
Sauces	
Sweets	
Ice cream	

(f) Why should you eat five times a day? Mention **two** things.   **2**

_____

_____

Total marks 10

Text 2

You come across this article in a Spanish magazine, all about exams.

Algunos consejos para los Exámenes

Venga preparado; debes llegar temprano para los exámenes y traer todos los materiales que necesitará, tales como lápices, calculadora, diccionario, y reloj. Esto le ayudará a tener todo a mano y concentrarse en la tarea.

Permanezca relajado y confiado. Recuérdese a sí mismo que está bien preparado y va a salir todo bien; si se siente ansioso antes o durante un examen, realice varias respiraciones lentas y profundas para relajarse. Va a ser mejor que no hables con otros estudiantes antes de un examen; la ansiedad es contagiosa.

Deberias utilizar un 10% de su tiempo de lectura leyendo toda el examen cuidadosamente, antes de empezar. A medida que lee las preguntas, escriba breves apuntes indicando ideas que podrá utilizar más tarde en sus respuestas. Planee contestar las preguntas fáciles primero y las preguntas más difíciles en último lugar, y contestar las preguntas del examen en un orden estratégico. Las últimas preguntas que responde deben ser las más difíciles, llevar la mayor cantidad de texto escrito, o tener el menor valor en puntaje. Resista el impulso a salir tan pronto ha completado todos los items. Asegúrese de haber contestado todas las preguntas de haber corrijido su escrito en cuanto a gramática y puntuación.

MARKS

Questions

(a) This advice is for: tick (✓) the correct box   1

Teachers organising exams	
Revising for exams	
What to do on the day of the exam	

(b) The first bullet point tells you what to bring. How will this help you? Complete the sentence.   2

This will help you _____, and to _____.

(c) In the second bullet point, you are given advice on what to do if you are anxious. What should you do? Why?   2

_____

_____

(d) Why should you not talk to other students before the exam?   1

_____

(e) What should you spend 10% of the time you have doing?   1

_____

(f) Which questions should you answer last? Mention **two** things.   2

_____

_____

(g) What temptation should you resist?   1

_____

Total marks 10

MARKS | DO NOT WRITE IN THIS MARGIN

Text 3

You read this article about a survey of public services which was carried out recently among young people in the province of Málaga.

Joven espíritu crítico

Más de setecientos alumnos de entre trece y dieciocho años han participado en una encuesta. Los resultados demuestran que los alumnos se preocupan sobre todo por el servicio de transporte urbano nocturno y las carreteras peligrosas por las que hay que pasar para ir a clase. Además se quejan de la ausencia de suficientes instalaciones deportivas fuera de las grandes ciudades.

Marisa

Para mí, sin lugar a dudas, lo que más me preocupa es la falta de seguridad por las calles del centro de la ciudad.

Felipe

En mi familia, intentamos reciclar lo más posible y nos hacen falta más contenedores para el reciclaje en nuestro barrio sin tener que andar kilómetros.

Antonia

Como mis compañeras de clase, me preocupan las antenas de telefonía móvil situadas cerca de nuestro instituto y sus posibles consecuencias peligrosas para la salud.

Diferencias entre ciudades y pueblos

La conclusión principal del sondeo es que existen diferencias importantes entre los servicios públicos puestos a disposición de los jóvenes según su lugar de residencia. Hay una clara desventaja para los que viven en pequeños pueblos. En muchos de los pueblos aislados, el único lugar de reunión para jóvenes es la plaza. Por otro lado, en las ciudades, aunque existen cines y discotecas, los jóvenes tienen problemas para volver a casa por la noche ya que no hay autobuses después de las doce.

Questions

    (a) Who exactly took part in this survey? Give details.   **1**

_____

    (b) What were they most concerned about? Give details about any **two** things.   **2**

_____

_____

    (c) What was Marisa most worried about?   **1**

_____

    (d) What recycling issue was Felipe concerned about?   **1**

_____

MARKS

Text 3 Questions (continued)

(e) What worried Antonia and her classmates? Tick (✓) the correct answers.   **2**

The mobile phone reception	
The mobile phone masts	
Health dangers	
The situation in her school	

(f) The survey reached the conclusion that there are important differences depending on where you live.

    (i) What disadvantage is there if you live in a remote village?   **1**

    _____

    (ii) What is the problem if you live in the city? Explain in detail.   **2**

    _____

    _____

Total marks 10

[END OF READING PAPER]

ADDITIONAL SPACE FOR ANSWERS

ADDITIONAL SPACE FOR ANSWERS

ADDITIONAL SPACE FOR ANSWERS

National Qualifications
MODEL PAPER 1

Spanish Writing

Duration — 1 hour and 30 minutes

Total marks — 20

WRITING — 20 marks

Write your answers clearly, in **Spanish**, in the space provided in this booklet.

You may use a Spanish dictionary.

Additional space for answers is provided at the end of this booklet.

Use **blue** or **black** ink.

There is a separate question and answer booklet for Reading. You must complete your answers for Reading in the question and answer booklet for Reading.

Before leaving the examination room you must give both booklets to the Invigilator; if you do not, you may lose all the marks for this paper.

HODDER GIBSON
LEARN MORE

MARKS

WRITING — 20 marks

You are preparing an application for the job advertised below and you write an e-mail in Spanish to the company.

Café en el centro de Malagá busca camarero/a

Necesitamos a una persona motivada, con conocimiento de español e inglés.

Para mas información, o si el empleo le interesa, debe ponerse en contacto con la Señora González a SGon@cafecentralmalaga.com.

To help you to write your e-mail, you have been given the following checklist of information to give about yourself and to ask about the job.

You must include all of these points:

- Personal details (name, age, where you live)
- School/college/education experience until now
- Skills/interests you have which make you right for the job
- Related work experience
- When you will be available for interview and to work
- Your experience of working with the public

Use all of the above to help you write the e-mail in Spanish. The e-mail should be approximately 120–150 words. You may use a Spanish dictionary.

ANSWER SPACE

ANSWER SPACE (continued)

ANSWER SPACE (continued)

MARKS

MARKS

ANSWER SPACE (continued)

[END OF WRITING PAPER]

ADDITIONAL SPACE FOR ANSWERS

MARKS

ADDITIONAL SPACE FOR ANSWERS

National Qualifications
MODEL PAPER 1

Spanish Listening

Duration — 25 minutes (approx)

Total marks — 20

When you are told to do so, open your paper.

You will hear two items in Spanish. **Before you hear each item, you will have one minute to study the question.** You will hear each item three times, with an interval of one minute between playings. You will then have time to answer the questions about it before hearing the next item.

Write your answers clearly, **in English**, in the spaces provided.

You may take notes as you are listening to the Spanish, but only in this booklet.

Use **blue** or **black** ink.

You may NOT use a Spanish dictionary.

You are not allowed to leave the examination room until the end of the test.

Before leaving the examination room you must give this booklet to the Invigilator. If you do not, you may lose all the marks for this paper.

MARKS | DO NOT WRITE IN THIS MARGIN

Item 1

Eduardo talks about his plans and the decisions he has to make about his future.

(a) What does he say about what he will study? Complete the sentence.   1

I would like to study _____.

(b) Why does he think that a gap year would be beneficial? Give **two** reasons.   2

_____

_____

(c) What problem does he have?   1

_____

(d) What solution has he found? Give exact details.   1

_____

(e) Why is he happy with this arrangement? Mention any **two** reasons.   2

_____

_____

(f) In your opinion, is Eduardo positive about his future prospects? Tick (✓) one box.   1

He is sure he is making the right choices	
He is worried he has not enough money	
He is not sure he should be planning to go to university	

Total marks   8

MARKS | DO NOT WRITE IN THIS MARGIN

Item 2

You are sitting in a swimming pool in Spain, listening to a conversation between one of your friends and Laura, a Spanish girl who is working there.

(a) Laura asks your friend two questions. What does she ask?   **2**

_____

_____

(b) What is Laura studying?   **1**

_____

(c) Laura worked in London. What did she do?   **1**

_____

(d) She tells what she thought of London. What did she not like? Mention **two** things.   **2**

_____ and _____

(e) She talks about why she likes her work. What does she say? Mention **two** things.   **2**

_____

_____

(f) What question does she ask your friend?   **1**

_____

_____

(g) She talks about some aspects of her work which are not so good. What does she say? Mention **two** things.   **2**

_____

_____

(h) She is going for a week's holiday in August. Who is she going with?   **1**

_____

Total marks 12

[END OF LISTENING PAPER]

[BLANK PAGE]

National
Qualifications
MODEL PAPER 1

Spanish
Listening Transcript

Duration — 25 minutes (approx)

(t)   Item number one.

Eduardo talks about his plans and the decisions he has to make about his future.

You now have one minute to study the question.

(m) Estoy en mi último curso en el colegio y lo que tengo muy claro es que quiero ir a la universidad. Voy a ser el primero de mi familia en hacerlo. Quisiera estudiar idiomas y relaciones internacionales pero también estoy considerando pasar un año sabático en otro país antes de empezar mis estudios en la universidad. Creo que podría ser una experiencia muy útil y beneficiosa ya que me daría la oportunidad de conocer otra cultura y de practicar los idiomas que he aprendido. El problema que tengo es que, como muchos estudiantes, no tengo mucho dinero y he tenido que buscarme un trabajo en un supermercado los fines de semana para ahorrar un poco. Estoy muy contento porque además de ganar dinero, me llevo muy bien con mi jefe y me lo paso estupendamente con los compañeros de trabajo. Se que tendré que trabajar en el futuro cuando sea estudiante, pero no es un problema para mí.

(2 minutes)

(t)   **Item number two.**

You are sitting in a swimming pool in Spain, listening to a conversation between one of your friends and Laura, a Spanish girl who is working there.

You now have one minute to study the question.

(m/f)   **¡Hola, señorita! ¿Qué tal?**

(f)   No sois de aquí ¿verdad? Pero hablas muy bien español. ¿Cuánto tiempo hace que lo estudias?

(m/f)   **Lo anos. ¡Gracias!**

(f)   A propósito, me llamo Laura y vivo aquí en Barcelona. Estudio ciencias naturales y ¡fíjate! después de las vacaciones voy a matricularme en la Universidad de Glasgow para continuar con mis estudios.

(m/f)   **¡Conozco bien Glasgow!**

(f)   ¿Sois de Inglaterra o de Escocia? El año pasado estuve en Londres. Trabajaba como asistente de español en un colegio en el centro de la ciudad. Me gustaba bastante pero no pude soportar lo sucias que eran las calles y lo malo que era el transporte público, sobre todo el metro.

(m/f)   **¿Trabajas aquí cada dia?**

(f)   No, trabajo a tiempo parcial. Como yo, muchos de mis compañeros trabajan. Como socorristas todo el verano. Me gusta el trabajo porque estoy al aire libre y conozco a mucha gente de distintos países. Además me encanta el mar.

(m/f)   **Trabajo en las vacaciones solamente.**

(f)   ¿Podéis decirme cuánto tiempo duran las vacaciones de verano? Me han dicho que son más cortas que en España.

(m/f)   **Duran siete semanas. ¿Entonces, te gusta tu trabajo?**

(f)   Sí, sin embargo no es todo de color de rosa. Me fastidia mucho tener que recoger toda la basura que tira la gente y las horas pueden resultar muy largas y a veces aburridas.

(m/f)   **¿Tienes vacaciones, este año?**

(f)   Sí, a finales de agosto mi mejor amiga y yo vamos a pasar un fin de semana en la costa. ¡Estoy impaciente! Vamos a descansar y, claro, a gastar mucho dinero. Ahora, tengo que irme al trabajo. Adiós.

(m/f)   **Adiós, Laura, y hasta luego.**

(2 minutes)

(t)   **End of test.**

Now look over your answers.

[END OF TRANSCRIPT]

Model Paper 2

Whilst this Model Paper has been specially commissioned by Hodder Gibson for use as practice for the National 5 exams, the key reference documents remain the SQA Specimen Paper 2013 and the SQA Past Papers 2014 and 2015.

National Qualifications
MODEL PAPER 2

Spanish Reading

Duration — 1 hour and 30 minutes

Total marks — 30

READING — 30 marks

Read all THREE texts and attempt ALL questions.

Write your answers clearly, in **English**, in the spaces provided in this booklet.

You may use a Spanish dictionary.

Additional space for answers is provided at the end of this booklet. If you use this space you must clearly identify the question number you are attempting.

Use **blue** or **black** ink.

There is a separate question and answer booklet for Writing. You must complete your answer for Writing in the question and answer booklet for Writing.

Before leaving the examination room you must give both booklets to the Invigilator; if you do not, you may lose all the marks for this paper.

MARKS | DO NOT WRITE IN THIS MARGIN

READING — 30 marks

Text 1

You read this piece of advice on how to get better marks at school.

¡A mejorar tus notas!

¿Te matas estudiando y aún así no sacas buenas notas?

Quizás la razón sea porque no estás estudiando bien. Aquí te presentamos algunos consejitos para que puedas mejorar tus calificaciones y celebrar a fin de curso.

Escucha bien a tu profesor, y no te pongas a dormir con los ojos abiertos ni a pensar en tu artista favorito. Los estudiantes que atienden al profesor generalmente necesitan estudiar menos en su casa. Además, con frecuencia los profesores dan durante la clase algunas indicaciones de lo que saldrá en el examen.

Concéntrarse es muy importente. Claro, si te has acostado tarde la noche anterior es un poco mas difícil. Muchos estudiantes duermen muy poco y por lo tanto en el salón de clase llega el sueño.

¿Qué pasa si te aburre tu profesor? Pues te lo tienes que aguantar. En la vida muchas veces tendrás que tolerar situaciones que no son entretenidas.

¡Cuidado con tus amigos! Si ellos tienen una actitud apática hacia la clase, te podrían contagiar. Piensa por ti mismo.

Finalmente, piensa en esto.

El ser humano es capaz de grandes cosas cuando se lo propone. Si piensas que no hay manera de que puedas sacar buenas notas en alguna clase, cambia esa manera de razonar. ¡Sé positivo!

Questions

(a) Why might your marks not be good, according to the article?   **1**

_____

(b) The article tells you two things which might stop you listening properly. What are they?   **2**

_____

MARKS | DO NOT WRITE IN THIS MARGIN

Text 1 Questions (continued)

(c) Why are you advised to listen carefully in class? Mention **two** things.   **2**

_____

_____

(d) Why might you find it sometimes difficult to concentrate in class?   **1**

_____

(e) What should you do if you find the teacher boring?   **1**

_____

(f) Why should you be careful with your friends?   **1**

_____

(g) What final advice are you given? Complete the phrases.   **2**

Human beings are capable of	
If you think you can't get better marks in a class,	

Total marks 10

MARKS

Text 2

Your friend in Spain tells you about a walk she is considering doing this summer and sends you an article about her plan.

Camino de Santiago Para Niños: una actividad diferente para las vacaciones

Esta información se ha elaborado para niños de 12 a 16 años de edad. Nuestras recomendaciones son las siguientes.

Preparación previa, mediante paseos cada vez más largos, con la mochila cargada y las botas que vayan a usarse durante el viaje y caminando sólo por la mañana. Levántate temprano para evitar las horas de más calor y anda hasta mediodía.

Es mejor no caminar muy rápido los primeros días, y adaptarte al ritmo del más lento del grupo. Valdré la pena tratar con amabilidad a la gente que encontrás al borde del camino, y hablar y compartir experiencias con otros peregrinos. Conocerás gente de todo el mundo. Los pelegrinos permiten el paso de los que anden más rápido. Recuerda que el camino no es una carrera y que no se trata de llegar el primero.

Será útil realizar etapas cortas, sobre todo los primeros días. Deberías parar cada hora de marcha para cinco minutos, aproximadamente, para descansar y tomar alimentos que proporcionen energía. En cuanto llegues al albergue, quítate las botas y ponte unas zapatillas para que descansen los pies.

Questions

(a) Who exactly is this activity aimed at? **1**

_____

(b) You are told what preparation you should undertake. Mention any **two** things. **2**

_____

_____

(c) (i) When should you walk? **1**

_____

(ii) Why should you do this? **1**

_____

(d) What should you do in the first days of the walk? Mention any **one** thing. **1**

_____

MARKS | DO NOT WRITE IN THIS MARGIN

Text 2 Questions (continued)

(e) Tick (✓) two pieces of advice the article gives.   2

Be nice to the people you meet on the road	
Be gentle with everybody	
Allow people to overtake	
Remember the path is not a road	

(f) What should you do when you reach the hostel? Why?   2

_____

_____

Total marks 10

Text 3

You find an article about how to encourage children to make the best use of their free time.

Las actividades extraescolares

No dependientes de la institución educativa son las actividades extraescolares programadas o improvisadas por las familias fuera de la jornada escolar, clases particulares, actividades deportivas, aprendizaje de idiomas, etc.

Son muchas las actividades que se les plantean a nuestros hijos como complemento de sus estudios. Realizar actividades extraescolares les permite aprender y divertirse a la vez. Si el niño es pequeño estará muy receptivo a aprender cosas nuevas porque lo vivirá como un juego.

El principal objetivo fuera del horario escolar debe ser fomentar su ocio, aunque si descubres que se encuentra cansado o no disfruta con ello debes darle la posibilidad de eligir otra ocupación que le guste más.

Deja que decida él la actividad que quiere hacer-no es conveniente que lo fuerces a hacer algo que a ti te apasiona. Lo ideal sería que eligiera una afición que le ayudara a olvidarse de la rutina diaria.

Sin embargo un exceso de actividades puede ser negativo ya que los niños pueden sentirse con tantas o más responsabilidades que una persona adulta.

No hay que olvidar que nuestros pequeños necesitan desconectar de las tareas escolares y disfrutar del cariño familiar.

Questions

(a) The article starts by mentioning some possible extracurricular activities for young people. Mention **two** of them.   2

_____

_____

MARKS

Text 3 Questions (continued)

(b) According to the article, what do extra-curricular activities allow a child to do? Complete the sentence.　　1

Extracurricular activities allow them to _____

_____ at the same time.

(c) Why will a younger child be keener on new things?　　1

_____

(d) What should you do if the child is not enjoying a particular activity?　　1

_____

(e) What type of activity is ideal?　　1

_____

(f) In what way could too many activities have a negative impact on a child?　　1

_____

(g) What should not be forgotten? Mention **two** things.　　2

_____

_____

(h) Who is this article written for? Tick (✓) the correct box.　　1

Teachers planning extracurricular activities	
Children and young people looking for things to do	
Parents of young people	

Total marks　10

[END OF READING PAPER]

ADDITIONAL SPACE FOR ANSWERS

Page seven

MARKS

DO NOT
WRITE IN
THIS
MARGIN

ADDITIONAL SPACE FOR ANSWERS

National Qualifications
MODEL PAPER 2

Spanish Writing

Duration — 1 hour and 30 minutes

Total marks — 20

WRITING — 20 marks

Write your answers clearly, in **Spanish**, in the space provided in this booklet.

You may use a Spanish dictionary.

Additional space for answers is provided at the end of this booklet.

Use **blue** or **black** ink.

There is a separate question and answer booklet for Reading. You must complete your answers for Reading in the question and answer booklet for Reading.

Before leaving the examination room you must give both booklets to the Invigilator; if you do not, you may lose all the marks for this paper.

MARKS DO NOT WRITE IN THIS MARGIN

WRITING — 20 marks

You are preparing an application for the job advertised below and you write an e-mail in Spanish to the company.

Colonia de Verano en Marbella

Buscamos personas entusiastas y llenas de energía para trabajar en nuestra organización en la costa del sol este verano.

Necesitamos jóvenes con conocimiento de español e inglés.

Para este puesto tiene que saber entenderse bien con los jóvenes.

Se deben organizar cursos de español o inglés, juegos, deportes y mucho más para un grupo de diez niños, de 5 a 13 años.

Contacto: enfocamp@enforex.es

To help you to write your e-mail, you have been given the following checklist of information to give about yourself and to ask about the job.

You must include all of these points:

- Personal details (name, age, where you live)
- School/college/education experience until now
- Skills/interests you have which make you right for the job
- Related work experience
- Which games, sports and activities you could help organise
- Your experience of working with young people

Use all of the above to help you write the e-mail in Spanish. The e-mail should be approximately 120–150 words. You may use a Spanish dictionary.

MARKS

DO NOT WRITE IN THIS MARGIN

ANSWER SPACE

ANSWER SPACE (continued)

ANSWER SPACE (continued)

MARKS | DO NOT WRITE IN THIS MARGIN

ANSWER SPACE (continued)

_____

_____

_____

_____

_____

_____

_____

_____

_____

_____

_____

_____

_____

_____

_____

_____

_____

_____

_____

_____

[END OF WRITING PAPER]

MARKS DO NOT WRITE IN THIS MARGIN

ADDITIONAL SPACE FOR ANSWERS

ADDITIONAL SPACE FOR ANSWERS

National
Qualifications
MODEL PAPER 2

Spanish
Listening

Duration — 25 minutes

Total marks — 20

When you are told to do so, open your paper.

You will hear two items in Spanish. **Before you hear each item, you will have one minute to study the question**. You will hear each item three times, with an interval of one minute between playings. You will then have time to answer the questions about it before hearing the next item.

Write your answers clearly, **in English**, in the spaces provided.

You may take notes as you are listening to the Spanish, but only in this booklet.

Use **blue** or **black** ink.

You may NOT use a Spanish dictionary.

You are not allowed to leave the examination room until the end of the test.

Before leaving the examination room you must give this booklet to the Invigilator. If you do not, you may lose all the marks for this paper.

HODDER
GIBSON
LEARN MORE

Item 1

You are in Madrid, and talk to Antonio, a Spanish student. He tells you about his job.

(a) What is Antonio's job?   1

_____

(b) Why does he like his job?   1

_____

(c) What does he say is a great advantage of this job? Complete the sentence.   1

A great advantage of the job is it allows me to _____.

(d) Antonio has had a summer job as a lifeguard for the past two years.

Why does he like this job? Give any **two** reasons.   2

_____

_____

(e) What does he like to do when he finishes work?   1

_____

(f) What problem does he sometimes have to deal with?   1

_____

(g) What does Antonio mainly talk about? Tick (✓) the correct box.   1

The sports he plays	
The work he does	
The problems he has	

Total marks   8

MARKS | DO NOT WRITE IN THIS MARGIN

Item 2

You are in Madrid on an exchange. One of your friends gets into conversation with a young Spanish student, while you are visiting a castle.

(a) He tells your friend he likes his work. Mention **one** reason.   **1**

_____

(b) He tells your friend about his ambitions. What are they? Mention **two** things.   **2**

_____

_____

(c) He tells you about his girlfriend. When did he meet her?   **1**

_____

(d) He tells you about her work. What does he say? Mention **two** things.   **2**

_____

(e) He asks your friend some questions. Give **two** of them.   **2**

_____

_____

(f) What does he say about young people working in Spain? Mention **two** things.   **2**

_____

_____

(g) He tells you he hopes to work in Central America when he has finished studying. What exactly does he intend to do? Mention **two** things.   **2**

_____

_____

Total marks 12

[END OF LISTENING PAPER]

[BLANK PAGE]

N5

National
Qualifications
MODEL PAPER 2

Spanish
Listening Transcript

Duration — 25 minutes (approx)

(t) Item number one.

Antonio tells you about his job.

You now have one minute to study the question.

(m) Siento una gran pasión por los deportes, ¡vamos! es que me encantan todo tipo de deportes. Soy profesor de educación física en un colégio en Nerja. Puedo decir sinceramente que me gusta muchísimo mi trabajo ya que estoy haciendo lo que me gusta y además cada día es diferente. Otra gran ventaja de este trabajo es que me permite mantenerme en forma.

También llevo dos veranos trabajando como socorrista en la playa de Nerja. Me gusta este trabajo porque me pagan bastante bien, sólo trabajo por las mañanas y tengo todos los miércoles libres. Y además, puedo encontrar a mucha gente de otros países, que es muy interesante. Cuando termino, me encanta ir a dar un paseo por la playa, a hablar con la gente.

No suele haber muchos problemas en mi trabajo sólo que a veces algún niño pequeño se pierde y no sabe dónde están sus padres. Así que tengo que hablar en inglés o en francés de vez en cuando.

(2 minutes)

(t)   **Item number two.**

You are in Madrid on an exchange. One of your friends gets into conversation with a young Spanish student, while you are visiting a castle.

You now have one minute to study the question.

(m/f)   ¡Hola! ¿Trabajas aquí?

Trabajo aquí a tiempo parcial. Me gusta mucho porque me pagan bien. Además, estudio arquitectura en la universidad y también me fascina la historia de esta región.

(m/f)   ¿Te gusta ser estudiante?

(m/f)   La educación es muy importante para mí. Cuando termine mis estudios, tengo la intención de trabajar en el extranjero. Siempre he querido hacerlo. En realidad el dinero no me interesa mucho. Lo que quiero es estar contento con mi trabajo y tal vez casarme algún día.

(m/f)   ¿Tienes una novia?

(m/f)   Sí, Elena y yo nos conocimos hace cuatro años. Los dos trabajábamos en la misma cafetería cuando estuve en el colegio.

(m/f)   ¿ Elena trabaja también?

(m/f)   Sí, Elena tiene un trabajo en una tienda en el pueblo, lo que le viene muy bien. Y tú ¿tienes algún trabajo a tiempo parcial o no te lo permiten tus estudios? ¿En Escocia se paga bien a los jóvenes? Yo creo que aquí no.

(m/f)   Sí, trabajo también en una tienda. Pero no pagan bien.

(m/f)   Dime, ¿en Escocia trabajan todos los estudiantes en verano? Aquí, sí. Y luego ¿a qué edad se permite tener un trabajo a tiempo parcial en Gran Bretaña? En España muchos chicos trabajan a los catorce años y no me parece bien.

(m/f)   Y me has dicho que vas a trabajar en el extranjero ¿verdad?

(m/f)   Como ya he dicho soy estudiante pero cuando termine mis estudios espero trabajar en Centroamérica. Hasta ahora nunca he estado fuera de España. Seré miembro de un equipo que va a reconstruir casas destrozadas por desastres naturales.

(2 minutes)

(t)   **End of test.**

Now look over your answers.

[END OF TRANSCRIPT]

Model Paper 3

Whilst this Model Paper has been specially commissioned by Hodder Gibson for use as practice for the National 5 exams, the key reference documents remain the SQA Specimen Paper 2013 and the SQA Past Papers 2014 and 2015.

HODDER
GIBSON
LEARN MORE

**National
Qualifications
MODEL PAPER 3**

**Spanish
Reading**

Duration — 1 hour and 30 minutes

Total marks — 30

SECTION 1 — READING — 30 marks

Read all THREE texts and attempt ALL questions.

Write your answers clearly, in **English**, in the spaces provided in this booklet.

You may use a Spanish dictionary.

Additional space for answers is provided at the end of this booklet. If you use this space you must clearly identify the question number you are attempting.

Use **blue** or **black** ink.

There is a separate question and answer booklet for Writing. You must complete your answer for Writing in the question and answer booklet for Writing.

Before leaving the examination room you must give both booklets to the Invigilator; if you do not, you may lose all the marks for this paper.

**HODDER
GIBSON**
LEARN MORE

MARKS

READING — 30 marks

Text 1

You read this report by Spanish school students about their visit to Aula 2013, the Universities' Open Day in Alicante.

Visita a "Aula 2013"

Entre los días doce y catorce de marzo tuvo lugar en Alicante el Salón Internacional del Estudiante, más conocido como "Aula". Como ya es habitual todos los años, se programó una visita a "Aula 2013" para los alumnos mayores, ya que pueden recibir toda la información que necesitan para su futuro educativo.

Lo que buscaban los estudiantes

La mayoría de los alumnos buscaban detalles concretos sobre determinados cursos de estudio, pero otros tantos anduvieron recogiendo folletos de todo tipo sin tener nada claro. Otra cosa muy solicitada fue la información sobre becas y las posibilidades de empleo de los distintos cursos de estudio.

Charlas informales pero informativas

Además de ver y recoger información, había la oportunidad de hablar con algunos profesores universitarios sobre sus cursos y de lo que ellos esperaban de sus estudiantes. También charlaron de manera más informal con algunos estudiantes universitarios de último curso para darles una idea de lo que ellos habían disfrutado más durante sus años en la universidad además de las dificultades que habían tenido que enfrentar.

También había posibilidades para divertirse

Pero los alumnos no sólo se dedicaban a informarse, sino que en "Aula" pudieron disfrutar de entretenimientos como, por ejemplo, partidas de tenis de mesa, guerras con balas de pintura y música en directo, con lo cual todos lo pasaron en grande.

Questions

(a) When exactly did the visit to "Aula 2013" take place?   1

_____

(b) Who was it intended for?   1

_____

(c) Why was it arranged?   1

_____

(d) What were most of the students looking for?   1

_____

MARKS | DO NOT WRITE IN THIS MARGIN

Text 1 Questions (continued)

(e) What else were the students keen to find out about? Mention **two** things.   **2**

_____

_____

(f) Which of the following statements are correct? Tick the correct boxes.   **2**

They could talk with professors about their courses	
The students could discuss their hopes	
They could talk with former students about their experiences	
They could talk about the difficulties of getting a loan	

(g) Some entertainment was also on offer. Mention any **two** examples.   **2**

_____

_____

Total marks 10

MARKS | DO NOT WRITE IN THIS MARGIN

Text 2

You read this article about green tourism, or eco tourism.

¿Qué es el Ecoturismo?

Te gustaría visitar lugares exóticos y conocer a los habitantes de tierras lejanas. Pero también te preocupa la conservación de la naturaleza. Tenemos la respuesta para ti: ecoturismo.

El término **ecoturismo** empezó a usarse hace cerca de treinta años, y ha sido sujeto de gran debate en cuanto a su definición. Actualmente el auténtico ecoturismo representa una opción viable de conservación del patrimonio natural y cultural de los pueblos, fomentando al mismo tiempo la noción de desarrollo económico sustentable.

¿Qué es un ecoturista?

Un ecoturista viaja para establecer contacto con la naturaleza, para disfrutarla y conocerla. El buen ecoturista no debería tirar basura, ni destrozar las plantas ni agredir a los animales. Debe aceptar y adaptarse a las condiciones que existen en cada sitio, sin tratar de alterarlas.

Hay que comprar productos locales para que se beneficien los habitantes del lugar donde se encuentra. El ecoturista es solidario con quienes necesitan ayuda.

¿Cómo se distingue el ecoturismo del turismo de naturaleza o el de aventura?

Para ser considerado ecoturismo, éste debe de involucrar mínimos impactos al medio ambiente, la participación activa de las comunidades locales, la educación para la conservación, y debe maximizar la derrama económica en la comunidad.

Questions

(a) According to the first paragraph of the article what might someone interested in ecotourism want to do? Mention **two** things.   2

_____

_____

(b) What might concern them?   1

_____

(c) (i) When, according to the article, did ecotourism start?   1

_____

(ii) What has been the subject of great debate?   1

_____

(d) Why does an ecotourist travel, according to the article?   1

_____

(e) What should they not do? Mention **one** thing.   1

_____

MARKS | DO NOT WRITE IN THIS MARGIN

Text 2 Questions (continued)

(f) The article mentions four things which are necessary in ecotourism. Complete any **three** items in the table.   3

Minimal impact on	
Active participation by	
Education	
Maximizing	

Total marks   10

Text 3

You read this piece of advice on employment.

¡La preparación lo es todo!

Es tu primer día de trabajo o de prácticas. Estás ante algo completamente nuevo. Primero tienes que intentar aprender el nombre de tus compañeros más cercanos, cuáles son los puestos de cada uno de ellos y quién es el director de cada departamento. Tienes también aprender cuáles son las tareas que tienes que hacer, y cuántas horas tienes que trabajar.

Este día es un día en el que tendrás que asimilar mucha información, mostrarte muy receptivo y prestar mucha atención a todo lo que te digan. Vale la pena tener siempre a mano un bloc de notas y un bolígrafo para escribir información esencial desde el horario de la cafetería hasta el código de seguridad de la puerta de acceso. Una vez escrito no tendrás que preocuparte por recordarlo y podrás centrar tu atención en otros asuntos.

Es aconsejable sonrir a la gente cuando se te presenten e intenta repetir su nombre en voz alta porque de esta forma te será mucho más fácil recordarlo. Te mostrarás como una persona positiva y vital, dispuesta a sacar adelante sus proyectos y saldrás airoso de tu primera experiencia.

Questions

(a) When should you be using this advice?   1

_____

(b) In the first paragraph, the writer mentions some things you should learn straight away. Choose any **two** and write them in English.   2

_____

_____

MARKS

Text 3 Questions (continued)

(c) As you have to absorb a lot of information, the article suggests you write things down. Why should you do this? Mention **two** things.

2

_____

_____

(d) What is the first thing you should do when people introduce themselves?

1

_____

(e) What else should you do at this time? Why?

2

_____

_____

(f) What should you show yourself to be? Mention **one** thing.

1

_____

(g) This article is intended for: tick (✓) one box.

1

People who have been unemployed	
Young people facing their first job	
A new boss meeting staff for the first time	

Total marks 10

[END OF READING PAPER]

ADDITIONAL SPACE FOR ANSWERS

ADDITIONAL SPACE FOR ANSWERS

National Qualifications
MODEL PAPER 3

Spanish Writing

Duration — 1 hour and 30 minutes

Total marks — 20

WRITING — 20 marks

Write your answers clearly, in **Spanish**, in the space provided in this booklet.

You may use a Spanish dictionary.

Additional space for answers is provided at the end of this booklet.

Use **blue** or **black** ink.

There is a separate question and answer booklet for Reading. You must complete your answers for Reading in the question and answer booklet for Reading.

Before leaving the examination room you must give both booklets to the Invigilator; if you do not, you may lose all the marks for this paper.

HODDER
GIBSON
LEARN MORE

MARKS

WRITING — 20 marks

You are preparing an application for the job advertised below and you write an e-mail in Spanish to the company.

Albergue juvenil Huelva

Se buscan jóvenes entusiastas y simpaticos para trabajar como empleados en la recepción de nuestro albergue del 30 mayo al 31 agosto.

Se necesitan jóvenes con conocimiento de español e inglés.

Es imprescindible tener buen trato con nuestros clientes, y ser muy organizado. El puesto también require colaborar en tareas de limpieza y orden.

Correo electronico: huelva.itj@juntadeandalucia.es

To help you to write your e-mail, you have been given the following checklist of information to give about yourself and to ask about the job.

You must include all of these points:

- Personal details (name, age, where you live)
- School/college/education experience until now
- Skills/interests you have which make you right for the job
- Related work experience
- How you can contribute to the day-to-day running of the hostel
- Your experience of travelling and visiting other countries.

Use all of the above to help you write the e-mail in Spanish. The e-mail should be approximately 120–150 words. You may use a Spanish dictionary.

ANSWER SPACE

ANSWER SPACE (continued)

MARKS | DO NOT WRITE IN THIS MARGIN

ANSWER SPACE (continued)

ANSWER SPACE (continued)

_____

_____

_____

_____

_____

_____

_____

_____

_____

_____

_____

_____

_____

_____

_____

_____

_____

_____

_____

_____

_____

_____

[END OF WRITING PAPER]

ADDITIONAL SPACE FOR ANSWERS

MARKS DO NOT WRITE IN THIS MARGIN

ADDITIONAL SPACE FOR ANSWERS

National Qualifications
MODEL PAPER 3

Spanish
Listening

Duration — 25 minutes

Total marks — 20

When you are told to do so, open your paper.

You will hear two items in Spanish. **Before you hear each item, you will have one minute to study the question.** You will hear each item three times, with an interval of one minute between playings. You will then have time to answer the questions about it before hearing the next item.

Write your answers clearly, **in English**, in the spaces provided.

You may take notes as you are listening to the Spanish, but only in this booklet.

Use **blue** or **black** ink.

You may NOT use a Spanish dictionary.

You are not allowed to leave the examination room until the end of the test.

Before leaving the examination room you must give this booklet to the Invigilator. If you do not, you may lose all the marks for this paper.

MARKS | DO NOT WRITE IN THIS MARGIN

Item 1

Luisa tells us about her family.

(a) What does Luisa say about her older brother? Mention any **one** thing.   1

_____

(b) What does she say about her dad's work? Mention any **one** thing.   1

_____

(c) What do they like to do as a family at weekends?   1

_____

(d) (i) What do they do once a month?   1

_____

(ii) Why does Luisa particularly enjoy this? Give any **one** reason.   1

_____

(e) What do they have arguments about? Mention any **two** things.   2

_____

_____

(f) In your opinion, is Luisa positive about relationships in her family? Tick (✓) the correct box.   1

Not at all	
Very much so	
Overall, yes	

Total marks   8

MARKS | DO NOT WRITE IN THIS MARGIN

Item 2

A Spanish exchange student, Clara, is giving an interview in your class. You listen to the interview carefully!

(a) Where exactly does Clara say she lives? Mention **two** things.   2

_____

_____

(b) She mentions a disadvantage of where she lives.

   (i) What is this?   1

   _____

   (ii) Why is this the case?   1

   _____

(c) When does she prefer to sit and read a book? Mention **two** things.   2

_____

_____

(d) Who does she go shopping with? When do they go? Give precise details.   2

_____

_____

(e) Which of the following statements are correct? Tick (✓) two boxes.   2

My grandfather lives with us	
My mother is blonde with green eyes	
My sister is very serious	
I get on well with her	

(f) Where does her friend Laura live?   1

_____

(g) Why do they get on well? Give **one** reason.   1

_____

Total marks 12

[END OF LISTENING PAPER]

[BLANK PAGE]

National Qualifications
MODEL PAPER 3

Spanish
Listening Transcript

Duration – 25 minutes (approx)

Instructions to reader(s):

For each item, read the English **once**, then read the Spanish **three times**, with an interval of 1 minute between the three readings. On completion of the third reading, pause for the length of time indicated in brackets after the item, to allow the candidates to write their answers.

Where special arrangements have been agreed in advance to allow the reading of the material, those sections marked **(f)** should be read by a female speaker and those marked **(m)** by a male; those sections marked **(t)** should be read by the teacher.

(t)　Item number one.

Luisa tells us about her family.

You now have one minute to study the question.

(f) En mi familia somos cinco personas—mis padres, mis dos hermanos y yo pero mi hermano mayor ya no vive con nosotros porque trabaja en otra ciudad. Mi padre es médico y trabaja muchas horas. Durante la semana llega bastante tarde a casa pero los fines de semana, nos gusta cenar todos juntos, en familia. Una vez al mes salimos a un pequeño restaurante italiano que hay cerca de nuestra casa y siempre lo pasamos muy bien. Me encanta cuando vamos allí porque todos estamos relajados, hablamos y nos reímos. Por otro lado, a veces no nos llevamos muy bien. Hay peleas por ejemplo sobre quién tiene que fregar los platos, sobre quién debe sacar al perro a pasear o sobre la hora a la que tenemos que estar en casa por la noche. Pero vamos, no es nada serio y por regla general somos amigos, y cuando hay problemas, sabemos encontrar soluciones a estos problemas hablando entre nosotros.

(2 minutes)

(t)   **Item number two.**

A Spanish exchange student, Clara, is being interviewed in your class. You listen to the interview carefully!

You now have one minute to study the question.

(m/f) **¡Hola, Clara! ¿Dime, dónde vives en España?**

(f)   Mi pueblo se encuentra a veinte kilómetros al sur de Valencia y está situado en una zona muy bonita.

(m/f) **¿Cómo es tu casa?**

(f)   Mi casa está en la parte más moderna del pueblo, al lado de la iglesia de San Pedro. El barrio es muy bonito pero lo que no me gusta es que hay mucho ruido, especialmente los domingos porque hay mucha gente.

(m/f) **¿Qué haces en tu tiempo libre en casa?**

(f)   En mi tiempo libre me gusta hacer muchas cosas diferentes, pero depende. Veo muy poco la tele, sólo a veces, si hay un partido de tenis importante o alguna película comedia. La verdad es que prefiero quedarme en casa y me siento en el sofá a leer un libro, si estoy cansada osi hace mal tiempo.

(m/f) **¿Y cuando sales?**

(f)   Cuando salgo, suele ser los sábados por la mañana con mi hermana mayor. En particular nos encanta ir a las tiendas de ropa que hay en el centro o a las zapaterías en la plaza mayor que siempre tienen mucha variedad.

(m/f) **¡Dime algo de tu familia! ¿Cuántos sois, por ejemplo?**

(f)   En mi familia somos cinco personas, mi padre, mi madre, mi hermana mayor y mi abuela. Mi madre se llama María, y es morena con los ojos verdes. Es baja y muy guapa. Mi padre se llama Juan, es alto y no tiene mucho pelo. Mi hermana Marta es muy tímida y es bastante seria pero me llevo bastante bien con ella. Mi abuela es muy simpática.

(m/f) **¿Puedes hablar de tus amigos?**

(f)   Tengo muchos amigos pero mi mejor amiga se llama Laura y vive cerca de mi casa. Tenemos los mismos gustos y compartimos las mismas aficiones como ir de compras, o nadar. ¡Nos llevamos estupendamente!

(m/f) **Gracias, Clara. Adiós.**

(f)   Gracias, hasta luego.

(2 minutes)

(t)   **End of test.**

Now look over your answers.

[END OF TRANSCRIPT]

NATIONAL 5

2014

FOR OFFICIAL USE

N5

National
Qualifications
2014

Mark

X769/75/01

Spanish
Reading

FRIDAY, 30 MAY
9:00 AM — 10:30 AM

Fill in these boxes and read what is printed below.

Full name of centre

Town

Forename(s)

Surname

Number of seat

Date of birth
Day   Month   Year

Scottish candidate number

Total marks — 30

Attempt ALL questions.

Write your answers clearly, in **English**, in the spaces provided in this booklet.

You may use a Spanish dictionary.

Additional space for answers is provided at the end of this booklet. If you use this space you must clearly identify the question number you are attempting.

Use **blue** or **black** ink.

There is a separate question and answer booklet for Writing. You must complete your answer for Writing in the question and answer booklet for Writing.

Before leaving the examination room you must give both booklets to the Invigilator; if you do not, you may lose all the marks for this paper.

MARKS | DO NOT WRITE IN THIS MARGIN

Total marks — 30

Attempt ALL questions

Text 1

You read an article about Erasmus – a grant for European university students.

Para muchos estudiantes universitarios, recibir una beca Erasmus es la mejor manera de compaginar los estudios con el deseo de viajar y vivir en otro país europeo. Son miles los estudiantes europeos que se han aprovechado de esta beca popular.

Casilda Chico, 23 años

"El impacto del programa Erasmus supuso un cambio enorme en mi vida. Al llegar a Bruselas en Belgica, descubrí una ciudad nueva, diferente a la mía. Además, estar en Bruselas me permitió visitar los alrededores, empaparme de otra cultura y pasármelo muy bien!".

Angela Durán, 30 años

"Yo me fui a Londres, Inglaterra. Aprendí infinidad de cosas nuevas, pero lo que más me gustó fue que volví a casa sabiendo hablar inglés, supe adaptarme a otro sistema educativo que el español y a relacionarme con otra serie de personas. Fue una experiencia impagable".

Santiago Arroyo, 30 años

"Pasé mi año en Venecia en Italia. Recuerdo que ningún día era igual que el anterior y que siempre había algo que hacer. No hay mejor sensación que la de ser estudiante en el extranjero y de ser capaz de desenvolverse en una ciudad desconocida y en otro idioma. La experiencia cambió mi manera de ver el mundo".

MARKS | DO NOT WRITE IN THIS MARGIN

Text 1 Questions

(a) For many university students, an Erasmus grant allows them to combine different things with studying. What are they?

2

_____

_____

(b) (i) For Casilda Chico, what was the impact of taking part in the Erasmus programme?

1

_____

(ii) According to Casilda, what were the advantages of studying in Brussels? State any **two** things.

2

_____

_____

(c) Give details of what Angela Durán liked most about her time spent studying in London. State any **two** things.

2

_____

_____

(d) (i) What does Santiago Arroyo remember about his year in Venice? State **two** things.

2

_____

_____

(ii) What did this experience change for him?

1

_____

_____

[Turn over

Text 2

You read a web article about the Mexican actor, Gael García Bernal.

Gael García Bernal

Featureflash/Shutterstock.com

Su carrera cinematográfica

El actor mexicano Gael García Bernal empezó su carrera artística actuando en el teatro y a la edad de once años actuó en su primera telenovela.

Desde entonces, Gael ha protagonizado las películas mexicanas más populares de los últimos tiempos y fue el protagonista de "Los diarios de motocicleta", película de gran éxito internacional que narró las aventuras de dos jóvenes argentinos que hacen un viaje en motocicleta por territorio suramericano. Su reciente película es una película política, pero también es graciosa y te emociona mucho.

Un gran activista social y político

Además, Gael es un gran activista social y político. Invierte mucho tiempo y energía en promover las campañas de Oxfam y en trabajar en defensa de la población más vulnerable.

Hace unos años, Gael visitó unas granjas en la región de Chiapas en México, donde descubrió lo difícil que era la vida para los granjeros. Ellos se quejan del sistema de comercio injusto.

La cumbre de las Naciones Unidas

Gael hizo un llamamiento a los líderes mundiales para combatir el cambio climático. Fue a la cumbre de las Naciones Unidas donde asistió a reuniones, discutió ideas, presentó estudios de casos, habló con los medios y entregó peticiones.

MARKS | DO NOT WRITE IN THIS MARGIN

Text 2 Questions

(a) How did Gael García Bernal's early career begin? State **two** things.   2

_____

_____

(b) The second paragraph tells us about two of his films.

    (i) How does the article describe Gael's film, "Los diarios de motocicleta"?   1

    _____

    (ii) How does the article describe Gael's **recent** film? State any **two** things.   2

    _____

    _____

(c) Gael is also a social and political activist. Complete the sentence.

He invests a lot of time and energy in _____

and in working for _____ .   2

(d) What did he find out when he visited Chiapas in Mexico?   1

_____

_____

(e) Gael went to the United Nations summit on climate change. What did he do there? State any **two** things.   2

_____

_____

[Turn over

Text 3

You read an article about job companies in Spain.

Las habilidades y competencias más buscadas por las empresas españolas

En el mundo laboral, existen ciertas habilidades y competencias importantes.

La informática

Tener conocimiento de las redes sociales es algo casi imprescindible en ámbitos como la publicidad, los negocios o la comunicación. Las empresas han prestado más atención a las redes sociales con el objetivo de lograr una buena reputación corporativa y para establecer contactos comerciales. Casi todas las profesiones tienen al menos un pequeño componente tecnológico y por eso, los empleados deberían saber utilizar bases de datos y buscar información por Internet.

Los idiomas

Las nuevas tecnologías han potenciado la importancia de más de una lengua. En España, el inglés se pone cada vez más útil porque gran parte de las aplicaciones y programas que utilizamos están en inglés.

Trabajadores proactivos

Las empresas valoran trabajadores con la capacidad de hacer frente a los problemas del día a día, con el deseo de comenzar nuevos proyectos y la habilidad de solucionar dificultades imprevistas.

El trabajo en equipo

Hoy en día las empresas están formadas por grandes equipos y los empleados tienen que trabajar juntos diariamente. Por lo tanto la capacidad de entenderse con los colegas es importante.

MARKS | DO NOT WRITE IN THIS MARGIN

Text 3 Questions

(a) According to the article, knowledge of social networks is extremely important in many areas. Name any **two** areas.   **2**

_____

_____

(b) What are the aims of companies that use social networks?   **2**

_____

_____

(c) What should most employees be able to do? Complete the sentence.

Most employees should be able to _____

and _____.   **2**

(d) The article goes on to talk about the importance of languages. Why is English becoming more useful in the world of work?   **1**

_____

(e) What do companies value in their employees? State any **two** things.   **2**

_____

_____

(f) In your opinion, what is the purpose of the article? Tick (✓) the correct box.   **1**

It gives you advice on how to find a job.	
It gives you advice on what skills you need in a job.	
It gives you advice on the best jobs to do.	

[END OF QUESTION PAPER]

MARKS | DO NOT WRITE IN THIS MARGIN

ADDITIONAL SPACE FOR ANSWERS

MARKS DO NOT WRITE IN THIS MARGIN

ADDITIONAL SPACE FOR ANSWERS

N5

National Qualifications 2014

Mark

X769/75/02

Spanish Writing

FRIDAY, 30 MAY

9:00 AM — 10:30 AM

Fill in these boxes and read what is printed below.

Full name of centre

Town

Forename(s)

Surname

Number of seat

Date of birth

Day   Month   Year

Scottish candidate number

Total marks — 20

Write your answer clearly, in **Spanish**, in the space provided in this booklet.

You may use a Spanish dictionary.

Additional space for answers is provided at the end of this booklet.

Use **blue** or **black** ink.

There is a separate question and answer booklet for Reading. You must complete your answers for Reading in the question and answer booklet for Reading.

Before leaving the examination room you must give both booklets to the Invigilator; if you do not, you may lose all the marks for this paper.

MARKS

Total marks — 20

You are preparing an application for the job advertised below and write an e-mail in **Spanish** to the company.

Buscamos recepcionista

Se necesita recepcionista para trabajar los fines de semana en un hotel en Madrid.

Preferiblemente con conocimientos básicos de inglés.   Hay posibilidad de alojamiento en el hotel.

Los interesados deben mandar un email al director del hotel: carmen.arroyolopez@hotelsol.es

---

To help you to write your e-mail, you have been given the following checklist.

You must include **all** of these points:

- Personal details (name, age, where you live)
- School/college/education experience until now
- Skills/interests you have which make you right for the job
- Related work experience
- Your plans for accommodation in Madrid
- Why you want to work in Madrid.

Use all of the above to help you write the e-mail in **Spanish**.   The e-mail should be approximately 120 — 150 words.   You may use a Spanish dictionary.

ANSWER SPACE

MARKS

_____

_____

_____

_____

_____

_____

_____

_____

_____

_____

_____

_____

_____

_____

_____

_____

_____

_____

_____

_____

_____

_____

_____

[Turn over

MARKS

DO NOT WRITE IN THIS MARGIN

ANSWER SPACE (continued)

MARKS | DO NOT WRITE IN THIS MARGIN

ANSWER SPACE (continued)

MARKS | DO NOT WRITE IN THIS MARGIN

ANSWER SPACE (continued)

[END OF QUESTION PAPER]

MARKS | DO NOT WRITE IN THIS MARGIN

ADDITIONAL SPACE FOR ANSWERS

MARKS | DO NOT WRITE IN THIS MARGIN

ADDITIONAL SPACE FOR ANSWERS

Page eight

N5

National Qualifications 2014

Mark

X769/75/03

Spanish Listening

FRIDAY, 30 MAY

10:50 AM — 11:15 AM (approx)

Fill in these boxes and read what is printed below.

Full name of centre

Town

Forename(s)

Surname

Number of seat

Date of birth

Day	Month	Year
D D	M M	Y Y

Scottish candidate number

Total marks — 20

Attempt ALL questions

Write your answers clearly, in **English**, in the spaces provided in this booklet. Additional space for answers is provided at the end of this booklet. If you use this space you must clearly identify the question number you are attempting.

Use **blue** or **black** ink.

You will hear two items in Spanish. **Before you hear each item, you will have one minute to study the questions.** You will hear each item three times, with an interval of one minute between playings. You will then have time to answer the questions before hearing the next item.

You may take notes as you are listening to the Spanish, but only in this booklet.

You may NOT use a Spanish dictionary.

You are not allowed to leave the examination room until the end of the test.

Before leaving the examination room you must give this booklet to the Invigilator; if you do not, you may lose all the marks for this paper.

MARKS | DO NOT WRITE IN THIS MARGIN

Total marks — 20

Attempt ALL questions

Item 1

Javier talks to us about whether or not he has a healthy lifestyle.

(a) What type of exercise does Javier do? State **two** things. **2**

_____

_____

(b) Why does he avoid fast food? State any **one** thing. **1**

_____

(c) Why does Javier's mum shop in the market? State any **one** thing. **1**

_____

(d) Javier has one weakness, however. What is it? Complete the sentence.

Javier's problem is that he loves _____ . **1**

(e) Why was Javier overweight when he was younger? State any **two** things. **2**

_____

_____

(f) How would you describe Javier's attitude towards his health? Tick (✓) the correct statement. **1**

He does lots to look after his health.	
He doesn't do much to look after his health.	
He doesn't care about his health.	

MARKS

Item 2

Sara talks to Javier about her lifestyle.

(a) What does Sara do to stay in shape? State any **one** thing.   **1**

_____

(b) What does she use her computer for? State any **two** things.   **2**

_____

_____

(c) What comment does Javier make about Sara's use of the computer?   **1**

_____

(d)   (i) Sara talks about her parents' opinion of social networks. Complete the sentence.

Sara's parents think that social networks can be dangerous because

_____ .   **1**

(ii) In what way does Sara avoid problems with social networks?

_____   **1**

(e) Why does she send a lot of texts? State any **one** thing.   **1**

_____

(f) What else does she do on her phone apart from texting? State any **two** things.   **2**

_____

_____

[Turn over

MARKS | DO NOT WRITE IN THIS MARGIN

2. (continued)

(g) Where does Sara go when she goes out? State **three** places.   3

_____

_____

_____

[END OF QUESTION PAPER]

ADDITIONAL SPACE FOR ANSWERS

ADDITIONAL SPACE FOR ANSWERS

National Qualifications 2014

X769/75/13

Spanish Listening Transcript

FRIDAY, 30 MAY

10:50 AM — 11:15 AM (approx)

This paper must not be seen by any candidate.

The material overleaf is provided for use in an emergency only (eg the recording or equipment proving faulty) or where permission has been given in advance by SQA for the material to be read to candidates with additional support needs. The material must be read exactly as printed.

Instructions to reader(s):

For each item, read the English once, then read the Spanish three times, with an interval of 1 minute between the three readings. On completion of the third reading, pause for the length of time indicated in brackets after the item, to allow the candidates to write their answers.

Where special arrangements have been agreed in advance to allow the reading of the material, those sections marked (f) should be read by a female speaker and those marked (m) by a male; those sections marked (t) should be read by the teacher.

(t)   **Item Number One**

Javier talks to us about whether or not he has a healthy lifestyle.

You now have one minute to study the questions.

(m) Primero, trato de llevar una vida sana. En general hago mucho ejercicio porque soy miembro de un equipo de baloncesto y también voy al gimnasio al menos una vez a la semana. Pienso que mi dieta es más o menos sana porque normalmente evito la comida rápida porque contiene mucha grasa y demasiada sal. Sé que tengo suerte porque todos los días, mi madre me prepara una cena equilibrada. Mi madre siempre hace la compra en el mercado para asegurarse que las verduras sean frescas y de buena calidad. Sin embargo, el problema es que me encantan las bebidas gaseosas – para mí son un verdadero placer pero sé que contienen demasiado azúcar. Hoy en día, me mantengo en forma, pero, cuando era niño, pesaba muchos más kilos. Me gustaba mucho la comida basura que ya no como nunca. Además, mis abuelos me daban pasteles cuando iba a visitarles a su casa. También, los fines de semana, mis amigos y yo solíamos comprar muchos caramelos con nuestro dinero.

(2 minutes)

(t) Item Number Two

Sara talks to Javier about her lifestyle.

You now have one minute to study the questions.

(m) Hola Sara, ¿qué haces para mantenerte en forma?

(f) ¡Hombre! No hago mucho para cuidarme la línea. A veces voy al polideportivo pero la verdad es que prefiero hacer otras cosas.

(m) ¡Ah vale! Entonces, ¿cómo prefieres pasar tus ratos libres?

(f) Uso mucho el ordenador en mi tiempo libre. Cuando vuelvo del instituto, me encanta conectarme para descargar las últimas canciones, chatear con amigos que no veo a menudo y a veces lo uso para buscar información para los deberes. Ya ves que lo encuentro útil.

(m) Claro que sí, pero me parece que pasas mucho tiempo usando el ordenador, ¿qué opinan tus padres?

(f) Mis padres se preocupan y dicen que las redes sociales pueden ser peligrosas porque mucha gente puede ver tu perfil. No estoy de acuerdo.

(m) Entonces, ¿qué piensas de eso?

(f) En mi opinión no hay ningún problema porque siempre mantengo mi perfil privado.

(m) ¡Buena idea! ¿Podrías vivir sin tu móvil?

(f) Pues no, porque lo necesito para mandar mensajes a mis amigos porque viven bastante lejos y no puedo salir mucho con ellos.

(m) Es una lástima. ¿Es un móvil inteligente?

(f) Sí, tengo un móvil nuevo y lo uso muchísimo. Aparte de mandar mensajes, leo páginas web sobre las personas famosas, y claro, muy a menudo, veo programas de televisión y, para organizarme, uso el calendario.

(m) Ah, yo también. Y cuando sales de casa, ¿adónde prefieres ir?

(f) Pues, siempre tengo que pasear el perro a lo largo de la playa todas las tardes, después del colegio. Los fines de semana, lo que más me gusta hacer es ir al centro comercial para ver lo que hay de nuevo en las tiendas. Cuando salgo con mis amigos, normalmente si hace buen tiempo tomamos unas copas en la plaza mayor.

(m) Pues nada, hasta la próxima.

(f) Vale, adiós.

(2 minutes)

(t) End of test.

Now look over your answers.

[END OF TRANSCRIPT]

[BLANK PAGE]

DO NOT WRITE ON THIS PAGE

N5

National Qualifications 2015

Mark

X769/75/01

Spanish Reading

FRIDAY, 29 MAY

9:00 AM – 10:30 AM

Fill in these boxes and read what is printed below.

Full name of centre

Town

Forename(s)

Surname

Number of seat

Date of birth

Day   Month   Year   Scottish candidate number

Total marks — 30

Attempt ALL questions.

Write your answers clearly, in **English**, in the spaces provided in this booklet.

You may use a Spanish dictionary.

Additional space for answers is provided at the end of this booklet. If you use this space you must clearly identify the question number you are attempting.

Use **blue** or **black** ink.

There is a separate question and answer booklet for Writing. You must complete your answer for Writing in the question and answer booklet for Writing.

Before leaving the examination room you must give both booklets to the Invigilator; if you do not, you may lose all the marks for this paper.

MARKS | DO NOT WRITE IN THIS MARGIN

TOTAL MARKS – 30

ATTEMPT ALL QUESTIONS

Text 1

You read an article about young people and part-time jobs.

TRABAJAR Y ESTUDIAR CON 16 AÑOS

Como joven es probable que tengas algún tiempo libre y el deseo de ganar dinero. Además de ofrecerte una fuente de ingresos para tus gastos personales, el primer empleo te permitirá independizarte, y ver cómo funciona el mundo de los negocios.

Un poco de dinero extra siempre viene bien para salir de juerga con los amigos y para ahorrar para el carné de conducir. Sin embargo, compaginar estudios y trabajo es un desafío para muchos que no tienen tiempo de terminar todos los deberes del instituto. Los trabajos típicos incluyen rellenar estantes en el supermercado, repartir periódicos en el barrio o cuidar niños de los parientes.

Natalia Méndez Goya, de dieciséis años, dice: «*Pues yo gano dinero extra enseñando a mi abuelo de setenta y tres años a utilizar internet y antes de ir al colegio paseo los dos perros de mi vecino.*»

Se recomienda que los jóvenes no trabajen de noche durante la semana porque les resultará muy difícil levantarse temprano por la mañana para llegar al instituto a tiempo. Entre los jóvenes que trabajan por la noche, muchos van a clase dormidos o sin haber tenido tiempo de desayunar y por lo tanto no aprenden prácticamente nada.

Questions

(a) Complete the following sentence.

As a young person you will probably have some free time and _____

_____ .

1

(b) What will your first job allow you to do? State any **one** thing.

_____

1

MARKS | DO NOT WRITE IN THIS MARGIN

Text 1 Questions (continued)

(c) How can you spend extra money? State **two** things.

2

_____

_____

(d) What jobs do young people typically do? Give details of any **two**.

2

_____

_____

(e) Natalia Méndez Goya talks about her part-time jobs. What does she do to earn extra money? State any **one** thing.

1

_____

_____

(f) (i) Why should young people not work at night?

1

_____

   (ii) What can happen to many young people who do work at night? State any **one** thing.

1

_____

(g) What does the article say about part-time jobs? Tick (✓) the correct box.

1

Having a part-time job while studying is something all young people should do.	
Having a part-time job while studying is difficult for many young people.	
Having a part-time job and studying is very popular in Spain.	

[Turn over

MARKS | DO NOT WRITE IN THIS MARGIN

Text 2

You read an article about a museum in Madrid.

El Museo de Arte Moderno

El Museo de Arte Moderno en Madrid va a celebrar su quinto aniversario con unas jornadas de puertas abiertas. Se podrán visitar, con acceso gratuito, las nuevas esculturas norteamericanas. Además, se ha creado una exposición de arte moderno europeo.

Dolores Rodríguez, directora del museo, informa: "estamos seguros de que ofrecemos una gran selección de arte que a todos los visitantes les va a apasionar. Al visitar el museo, la gente puede descubrir a artistas menos conocidos además de mirar pinturas de los últimos cincuenta años."

El público también tendrá la oportunidad de participar en la celebración votando por su obra de arte favorita. Pueden dar su opinión a través de las pantallas táctiles en las salas del museo o rellenando una encuesta en la página web.

El horario será el habitual de lunes a sábado, de diez a siete horas de la tarde. Si las jornadas tienen mucho éxito, Dolores tiene planes de organizar más días de acceso gratuito para los jubilados.

Questions

(a) Which anniversary is the museum celebrating?

_____

1

(b) The museum is having a series of open days. What will people be able to visit? State **two** things.

_____

_____

2

MARKS | DO NOT WRITE IN THIS MARGIN

Text 2 Questions (continued)

(c) Dolores Rodríguez says the museum offers a large selection of art. According to Dolores, what will visitors think of it?   **1**

_____

(d) What can people do during their visit? Complete the sentence.   **2**

People can discover _____ and

they can look at paintings _____ .

(e) The public is encouraged to participate in the museum's anniversary.

   (i) How can they take part in the celebration?   **1**

     _____

     _____

   (ii) How will they be able to give their opinion? State **two** things.   **2**

     _____

     _____

(f) What plans does Dolores have for the museum?   **1**

_____

_____

[Turn over

MARKS | DO NOT WRITE IN THIS MARGIN

Text 3

You read an article about facial recognition software which is being developed for use in cars.

El reconocimiento facial dentro del coche

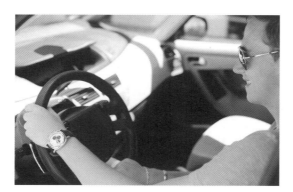

La mayor parte de los accidentes de tráfico son debidos al conductor, por ejemplo si el conductor conduce con un exceso de velocidad o sin prudencia. Así que no es de extrañar que cada vez más fabricantes de automóviles trabajen en el desarrollo de una tecnología que emplea una cámara de vídeo y un *software* de reconocimiento facial para intentar mejorar la seguridad durante la conducción.

La cámara grabará los cambios de las expresiones faciales, movimientos musculares, y emociones del rostro del conductor. Además, el sistema tendrá que estar permanentemente vigilante para poder reconocer si el conductor está distraído, si está sufriendo somnolencia o si no está en condiciones de seguir conduciendo.

Hay alguna dificultad. Hay que buscar la mejor posición para la cámara para que tenga una buena visión del rostro del conductor.

Este sistema puede advertir al conductor de que no está en condiciones para conducir por hacer sonar una alarma cinco veces si está durmiendo.

No cabe duda alguna de que reducir los riesgos al factor humano de una manera tecnológica es positivo. Por ejemplo, puede ayudar al conductor a actuar para evitar un accidente.

Questions

    (a) Complete the following sentence.   2

        Most traffic accidents are the fault of the driver. For example if the driver

        is driving _____ or _____ .

MARKS | DO NOT WRITE IN THIS MARGIN

Text 3 Questions (continued)

(b) What is the purpose of facial recognition software in cars?   **1**

_____

_____

(c) What will the camera record? State any **two** things.   **2**

_____

_____

(d) Why will the system have to be permanently switched on? State any **two** things.   **2**

_____

_____

(e) How can the system warn drivers? Give **two** details.   **2**

_____

_____

(f) According to the final paragraph, why is this type of technology positive?   **1**

_____

_____

[END OF QUESTION PAPER]

MARKS DO NOT WRITE IN THIS MARGIN

ADDITIONAL SPACE FOR ANSWERS

ADDITIONAL SPACE FOR ANSWERS

[BLANK PAGE]

DO NOT WRITE ON THIS PAGE

N5

National Qualifications 2015

Mark

X769/75/02

Spanish Writing

FRIDAY, 29 MAY

9:00 AM – 10:30 AM

Fill in these boxes and read what is printed below.

Full name of centre

Town

Forename(s)

Surname

Number of seat

Date of birth

Day   Month   Year   Scottish candidate number

Total marks — 20

Write your answer clearly, in **Spanish**, in the space provided in this booklet.

You may use a Spanish dictionary.

Additional space for answers is provided at the end of this booklet.

Use **blue** or **black** ink.

There is a separate question and answer booklet for Reading. You must complete your answers for Reading in the question and answer booklet for Reading.

Before leaving the examination room you must give both booklets to the Invigilator; if you do not, you may lose all the marks for this paper.

MARKS DO NOT WRITE IN THIS MARGIN

TOTAL MARKS - 20

You are preparing an application for the job advertised below and you write an e-mail in **Spanish** to the company.

Se necesita dependiente/dependienta

Se requiere una persona seria, dinámica y responsable para trabajar en una tienda de ropa en Sevilla.

Imprescindible hablar inglés y preferiblemente otro idioma. Buena presencia esencial.

Se ruega escribir al director de la tienda:
manuel.garciaramirez@tiendaroja.es

To help you to write your e-mail, you have been given the following checklist.

You must include **all** of these points:

- Personal details (name, age, where you live)
- School/college/education experience until now
- Skills/interests you have which make you right for the job
- Related work experience
- Languages spoken
- Reasons for application

Use all of the above to help you write the e-mail in **Spanish**. The e-mail should be approximately 120–150 words. You may use a Spanish dictionary.

ANSWER SPACE

[Turn over

ANSWER SPACE (continued)

MARKS DO NOT WRITE IN THIS MARGIN

ANSWER SPACE (continued)

[Turn over

MARKS | DO NOT WRITE IN THIS MARGIN

ANSWER SPACE (continued)

_____

_____

_____

_____

_____

_____

_____

_____

_____

_____

_____

_____

_____

_____

_____

_____

_____

_____

_____

[END OF QUESTION PAPER]

MARKS | DO NOT WRITE IN THIS MARGIN

ADDITIONAL SPACE FOR ANSWERS

MARKS | DO NOT WRITE IN THIS MARGIN

ADDITIONAL SPACE FOR ANSWERS

FOR OFFICIAL USE

N5

National
Qualifications
2015

Mark ☐

X769/75/03

**Spanish
Listening**

FRIDAY, 29 MAY

10:50 AM – 11:15 AM (approx)

Fill in these boxes and read what is printed below.

Full name of centre

Town

Forename(s)

Surname

Number of seat

Date of birth

Day   Month   Year   Scottish candidate number

Total marks — 20

Attempt ALL questions.

You will hear two items in Spanish. **Before you hear each item, you will have one minute to study the questions.** You will hear each item three times, with an interval of one minute between playings. You will then have time to answer the questions before hearing the next item.

You may NOT use a Spanish dictionary.

Write your answers clearly, in **English**, in the spaces provided in this booklet. Additional space for answers is provided at the end of this booklet. If you use this space you must clearly identify the question number you are attempting.

Use **blue** or **black** ink.

You are not allowed to leave the examination room until the end of the test.

Before leaving the examination room you must give this booklet to the Invigilator; if you do not, you may lose all the marks for this paper.

MARKS | DO NOT WRITE IN THIS MARGIN

Total marks — 20

Attempt ALL questions

Item 1

Luisa talks about languages.

(a) What does Luisa say about her mum? State any **one** thing.

_____

1

(b) What makes Luisa's English classes fun? State any **one** thing.

_____

1

(c) Apart from computers, what other kind of technology does she use in her English class?

_____

1

(d) Luisa talks about the advantage of speaking different languages. What does she say?

_____

1

(e) Luisa went to a summer camp last year. Where did she go?

_____

1

(f) What does she want to do when she finishes her studies? State **two** things.

_____

_____

2

(g) Which statement best matches Luisa's attitude to languages? Tick (✓) the correct statement.

1

She really likes them but they are just another school subject.	
She thinks they are good for holidays.	
They play an important part in many areas of her life.	

Item 2

Francisco talks to Luisa about his exams.

		MARKS	DO NOT WRITE IN THIS MARGIN

(a) How much time does Francisco spend revising?

    1

_____

(b) He gives details of the exam timetable. Tick (✓) the **two** correct statements.

    2

The exams start the next day.	
The first exam is Biology.	
The exams finish on the 12th of June.	
They last for 17 days in total.	

(c) Why does he prefer studying with a friend? State any **two** things.

    2

_____

_____

(d) How does he relax when he has a break? State any **two** things.

    2

_____

_____

(e) What does he find difficult about History?

    1

_____

(f) Francisco says the weather is nice. What would he rather be doing? State any **two** things.

    2

_____

_____

(g) Francisco is anxious about his Maths exam. Why? State any **two** things.

    2

_____

_____

[END OF QUESTION PAPER]

ADDITIONAL SPACE FOR ANSWERS

ADDITIONAL SPACE FOR ANSWERS

MARKS | DO NOT WRITE IN THIS MARGIN

[BLANK PAGE]

DO NOT WRITE ON THIS PAGE

N5

National
Qualifications
2015

X769/75/13

Spanish
Listening Transcript

FRIDAY, 29 MAY
10:50 AM – 11:15 AM (approx)

This paper must not be seen by any candidate.

The material overleaf is provided for use in an emergency only (eg the recording or equipment proving faulty) or where permission has been given in advance by SQA for the material to be read to candidates with additional support needs. The material must be read exactly as printed.

Instructions to reader(s)

For each item, read the English **once**, then read the Spanish **three times**, with an interval of 1 minute between the three readings. On completion of the third reading, pause for the length of time indicated in brackets after the item, to allow the candidates to write their answers.

Where special arrangements have been agreed in advance to allow the reading of the material, those sections marked **(f)** should be read by a female speaker and those marked **(m)** by a male; those sections marked **(t)** should be read by the teacher.

(t)   **Item Number One**

Luisa talks about languages.

You now have one minute to study the questions for Item Number One.

(f)   Siempre me han interesado los idiomas. Creo que es porque mi madre es suiza y habla muchas lenguas . . . francés, italiano y alemán.

Además, este año tengo suerte porque en el colegio tenemos una profesora de inglés que es muy entusiasta. Sus clases son muy divertidas – aprendemos canciones y ella tiene muy buen sentido del humor. También, utilizo la tecnología a menudo, es decir los ordenadores y la pizarra interactiva así que las clases son muy interesantes. Una ventaja de aprender lenguas es que puedo ayudar a muchos de los turistas extranjeros que visitan mi ciudad cada año.

El año pasado pasé un mes en un campamento de verano en la costa este de Irlanda – me lo pasé de maravilla y mi inglés ha mejorado mucho.

He decidido que cuando termine mis estudios quisiera encontrar trabajo en una empresa internacional y viajar por todo el mundo.

Lo tengo muy claro, todos los jóvenes deberían hablar una lengua además de la materna.

(2 minutes)

(t) **Item Number Two**

Francisco talks to Luisa about his exams.

You now have one minute to study the questions for Item Number Two.

(f) Hace mucho que no te veo, Francisco . . . ¿qué tal?

(m) En este momento estoy preparando mis exámenes de fin de curso. Cada tarde paso tres horas repasando mis asignaturas.

(f) Y ¿cuándo son estos exámenes?

(m) Empiezan el martes por la mañana . . . el primero es biología. Terminan el 11 de junio con informática. Así que en total duran 17 días. ¡Qué tostón!

(f) No es fácil trabajar solo ¿verdad?

(m) Tienes razón, pero a veces mi amigo Vicente viene a mi casa y trabajamos juntos, creo que aprendo mejor, el tiempo pasa más rápido y no me aburro tanto.

(f) Pero es importante también tomarse un descanso de vez en cuando ¿no?

(m) Sí, sí . . . me tomo un descanso cada hora para comer unas galletas, llamar a mis amigos o mirar una telenovela durante diez minutos . . . depende.

(f) Y estudiar ¿te parece fácil?

(m) Para mí lo más difícil es la historia, me cuesta mucho memorizar las fechas importantes.

(f) Sí . . . pero creo que es igual para todo el mundo.

(m) Lo peor es que en este momento hace buen tiempo y me gustaría estar al aire libre para dar una vuelta en bici o entrenarme con mi club de natación. Pero no hay más remedio.

(f) Bueno, por lo menos pareces muy relajado.

(m) ¡No! El miércoles tengo exámen de matemáticas. Estoy un poco preocupado porque creo que no he trabajado bastante en clase. Además, no me siento muy bien y me duele un poco la garganta. ¡Ojalá que todo salga bien!

(2 minutes)

(t) **End of test.**

Now look over your answers.

[END OF TRANSCRIPT]

[BLANK PAGE]

DO NOT WRITE ON THIS PAGE

NATIONAL 5 | ANSWER SECTION

SQA AND HODDER GIBSON NATIONAL 5 SPANISH 2015

NATIONAL 5 SPANISH
MODEL PAPER 1

Reading

Text 1

(a) • Eat food low in saturated fat(and in cholestorol)
     • Limit sugar and salt
     • Eat more food with fibre
     • Eat fruit, vegetables and cereal products
     Any two of the above

(b) Don't stop eating

(c) • Drink lots of water
     • Water is an essential nutrient
     • You don't have to feel thirsty to drink
     Any one of the above

(d) • You will be hungry all day
     • You will eat more

(e) You are given advice on what kind of food to avoid. Tick (✓) the correct boxes.

Big salads	
Sauces	✓
Sweets	✓
Ice cream	

(f) • It's better for your stomach
     • Better for your brain
     • Will stop you eating between meals
     Any two of the above

Text 2

(a) This advice is for: tick (✓) the correct box

Teachers organising exams	
Revising for exams	✓
What to do on the day of the exam	

(b) This will help you to have everything ready to hand, and to concentrate on the task

(c) • Take some (slow) deep breaths
     • In order to relax

(d) • Anxiety (or worry) is catching (or contagious)

(e) • Reading the exam carefully (before you start)

(f) • The hardest questions
     • The ones with most text
     • The ones with least marks
     Any two of the above

(g) Leave the exam before you have finished

Text 3

(a) • More than 600 pupils
     • Between 13–18 years old
     Any one of the above

(b) • Transport in towns at night
     • Dangerous roads to get to school
     • Lack of sporting facilities outside big towns
     Any two of the above

(c) Lack of safety in streets in town

(d) The need for more recycling containers (so they don't have to go a long distance to reach them)

(e) What worried Antonia and her classmates? Tick (✓) the correct answers.

The mobile phone reception	
The mobile phone masts	✓
Health dangers	✓
The situation in her school	

(f) (i) The only place to meet is the village/town square
     (ii) • They have difficulties getting home at night
         • There are no buses **after midnight**

Writing

Candidates will write a piece of extended writing in the modern language by addressing six bullet points. These bullet points will follow on from a job-related scenario. The bullet points will cover the four contexts of society, learning, employability and culture to allow candidates to use and adapt learned material. The first four bullet points will be the same each year and the last two will change to suit the scenario. Candidates need to address these "unpredictable bullet points" in detail to access the full range of marks.

Category	Mark	Content	Accuracy	Language resource — variety, range, structures
Very good	20	The job advert has been addressed in a full and balanced way. The candidate uses detailed language. The candidate addresses the advert completely and competently, **including information in response to both unpredictable bullet points.** A range of verbs/verb forms, tenses and constructions is used. Overall this comes over as a competent, well thought-out and serious application for the job.	The candidate handles all aspects of grammar and spelling accurately, although the language may contain one or two minor errors. Where the candidate attempts to use language more appropriate to Higher, a slightly higher number of inaccuracies need not detract from the overall very good impression.	The candidate is comfortable with the first person of the verb and generally uses a different verb in each sentence. Some modal verbs and infinitives may be used. There is good use of adjectives, adverbs and prepositional phrases and, where appropriate, word order. There may be a range of tenses. The candidate uses co-ordinating conjunctions and/or subordinate clauses where appropriate. The language of the e-mail flows well.
Good	16	The job advert has been addressed competently. There is less evidence of detailed language. The candidate uses a reasonable range of verbs/verb forms. Overall, the candidate has produced a genuine, reasonably accurate attempt at applying for the specific job, **even though he/she may not address one of the unpredictable bullet points.**	The candidate handles a range of verbs fairly accurately. There are some errors in spelling, adjective endings and, where relevant, case endings. Use of accents is less secure, where appropriate. Where the candidate is attempting to use more complex vocabulary and structures, these may be less successful, although basic structures are used accurately. There may be one or two examples of inaccurate dictionary use, especially in the unpredictable bullet points.	There may be repetition of verbs. There may be examples of listing, in particular when referring to school/college experience, without further amplification. There may be one or two examples of a co-ordinating conjunction, but most sentences are simple sentences. The candidate keeps to more basic vocabulary, particularly in response to either or both unpredictable bullet points.

Category	Mark	Content	Accuracy	Language resource — variety, range, structures
Satisfactory	12	The job advert has been addressed fairly competently. The candidate makes limited use of detailed language. The language is fairly repetitive and uses a limited range of verbs and fixed phrases, eg *I like, I go, I play*. The candidate copes fairly well with areas of personal details, education, skills, interests and work experience but does not deal fully with the two unpredictable bullet points **and indeed may not address either or both of the unpredictable bullet points.** On balance however the candidate has produced a satisfactory job application in the specific language.	The verbs are generally correct, but may be repetitive. There are quite a few errors in other parts of speech — gender of nouns, cases, singular/plural confusion, for instance. Prepositions may be missing, eg *I go the town.* Overall, there is more correct than incorrect.	The candidate copes with the first and third person of a few verbs, where appropriate. A limited range of verbs is used. Sentences are basic and mainly brief. There is minimal use of adjectives, probably mainly after *is* eg *Chemistry is interesting.* The candidate has a weak knowledge of plurals. There may be several spelling errors, eg reversal of vowel combinations.
Unsatisfactory	8	The job advert has been addressed in an uneven manner and/or with insufficient use of detailed language. The language is repetitive, eg *I like, I go, I play* may feature several times. There may be little difference between Satisfactory and Unsatisfactory. **Either or both of the unpredictable bullet points may not have been addressed.** There may be one sentence which is not intelligible to a sympathetic native speaker.	Ability to form tenses is inconsistent. There are errors in many other parts of speech — gender of nouns, cases, singular/plural confusion, for instance. Several errors are serious, perhaps showing mother tongue interference. The detail in the unpredictable bullet points may be very weak. Overall, there is more incorrect than correct.	The candidate copes mainly only with the personal language required in bullet points 1 and 2. The verbs "is" and "study" may also be used correctly. Sentences are basic. An English word may appear in the writing. There may be an example of serious dictionary misuse.

Category	Mark	Content	Accuracy	Language resource — variety, range, structures
Poor	4	The candidate has had considerable difficulty in addressing the job advert. There is little evidence of the use of detailed language. Three or four sentences may not be understood by a sympathetic native speaker. **Either or both of the unpredictable bullet points may not have been addressed.**	Many of the verbs are incorrect. There are many errors in other parts of speech — personal pronouns, gender of nouns, cases, singular/plural confusion, prepositions, for instance. The language is probably inaccurate throughout the writing.	The candidate cannot cope with more than one or two basic verbs. The candidate displays almost no knowledge of the present tense of verbs. Verbs used more than once may be written differently on each occasion. Sentences are very short. The candidate has a very limited vocabulary. Several English words may appear in the writing. There are examples of serious dictionary misuse.
Very poor	0	The candidate is unable to address the job advert. **The two unpredictable bullet points may not have been addressed.** Very little is intelligible to a sympathetic native speaker.	Virtually nothing is correct.	The candidate may only cope with the verbs *to have* and *to be*. Very few words are written correctly in the modern language. English words are used. There may be several examples of mother tongue interference. There may be several examples of serious dictionary misuse.

NATIONAL 5 SPANISH MODEL PAPER 1

Listening

Item 1

(a) Languages (with international relations)

(b) • He could get to know another culture
• Practise the languages he has learned

(c) He does not have much money

(d) He works in a supermarket **at the weekend**

(e) • He earns money
• Gets on with his boss
• Gets on really well with his colleagues
Any two of the above

(f) In your opinion, is Eduardo positive about his future prospects? Tick (✓) one box.

He is sure he is making the right choices	✓
He is worried he has not enough money	
He is not sure he should be planning to go to university	

Item 2

(a) • You're not from here, are you?
• How long have you been learning Spanish?

(b) Biology (and geology) or natural sciences

(c) She was a (Spanish) assistant in a school

(d) She couldn't stand **how dirty the streets were**, and also how bad the **public transport** was.

(e) • Her work is outside (in the open air)
• She meets people from different countries
• She loves the sea
Any two of the above

(f) How long are your summer holidays?

(g) • She has to collect litter people throw away
• It can be long hours
• Boring sometimes
Any two of the above

(h) Her **best** friend

NATIONAL 5 SPANISH MODEL PAPER 2

Reading

Text 1

(a) You are not studying properly

(b) • Going **to sleep with your eyes open**
• Thinking about **your favourite artist.**

(c) • People who listen to their teacher have to study less
• You might get hints about what is in the exam

(d) • You have stayed up too late
• You haven't slept enough
Any one of the above

(e) Learn to live with it

(f) If they have an apathetic (negative) attitude, it can be catching (infectious)

(g) What final advice are you given? Complete the phrases.

Human beings are capable of	**great things when they try**
If you think you can't get better marks in a class,	**change your way of thinking**

Text 2

(a) Young people **between 12 and 16.**

(b) • Take longer and longer walks
• With a full bag
• Wearing the shoes you will wear for the walk
Any one of the above

(c) (i) In the morning (or before midday)
(ii) To avoid the hottest time of day

(d) • Don't walk too fast
• Go at the pace of the slowest
Any one of the above

(e) Tick (✓) two pieces of advice the article gives.

Be nice to the people you meet on the road	✓
Be gentle with everybody	
Allow people to overtake	✓
Remember the path is not a road	

(f) • Take off your boots
• To allow your feet to rest

Text 3

(a) • Individual lessons
• Sporting activities
• Learning languages
Any two of the above

(b) Extracurricular activities allow them to **learn** and be **entertained** at the same time (both words needed).

(c) They will see it as a game.

(d) Give them the chance to try something else.

(e) Something that lets them forget their daily routine.

(f) They can feel they have the responsibilities of an adult.

(g) Get away from the school routine/enjoy family affection

(h) Who is this article written for? Tick (✓) the correct box.

Teachers planning extracurricular activities	
Children and young people looking for things to do	
Parents of young people	✓

Writing

Please see the assessment criteria for Writing on pages 148 to 150.

NATIONAL 5 SPANISH MODEL PAPER 2

Listening

Item 1

(a) He is a PE teacher

(b) • He is doing something he likes
    • Everyday is different
    Any one of the above

(c) A great advantage of the job is it allows me to **keep fit**.

(d) • It is well paid
    • He only works in the mornings
    • He has Wednesdays free
    • He can meet lots of people from other countries
    Any two of the above

(e) • Go for a walk on the beach
    • Talk to people on the beach
    Any one of the above

(f) • Lost children
    • Children who don't know where their parents are

(g) What does Antonio mainly talk about? Tick (✓) the correct box.

The sports he plays	
The work he does	✓
The problems he has	

Item 2

(a) • It is well paid
    • He is studying architecture and is interested in history of the region
    Any one of the above

(b) • Work abroad
    • Be happy in his work
    • Get married some day
    Any two of the above

(c) Four years ago

(d) Elena has **a job in a shop**, which **she likes (suits her)**.

(e) • Do you have a part-time job?
    • Are young people paid well?
    • Do Scottish students work in the summer?
    • How old do you have to be to get a part-time job?
    Any two of the above

(f) They start work at **fourteen**, he does not think this is good

(g) • Be member of a team
    • Which rebuilds houses
    • Destroyed by natural disasters
    Any two of the above

NATIONAL 5 SPANISH
MODEL PAPER 3

Reading

Text 1

(a) From the **12th** to the **14th** of **March**

(b) **Older** pupils

(c) To give them information about their future education

(d) Looked for details about specific courses

(e) • The possibility of bursaries (grants)
   • The possibilities for work the courses offered

(f) Which of the following statements are correct?

They could talk with professors about their courses	✓
The students could discuss their hopes	
They could talk with former students about their experiences	✓
They could talk about the difficulties of getting a loan	

(g) • Table tennis
   • Paint balling
   • Live music
   Any two of the above

Text 2

(a) • Visit exotic places
   • Get to know people who live far away

(b) Preserving nature (the environment)

(c) (i) About 30 years ago
   (ii) How it is defined/what its definition is

(d) To get in touch with nature

(e) • Throw away rubbish
   • Destroy plants
   • Hurt animals
   Any one of the above

(f) The article mentions four things which are necessary in ecotourism. Complete the table.

Minimal impact on	the environment
Active participation by	the local community
Education	for conservation
Maximizing	economic advantage in the community

Text 3

(a) • Your first day at work
   • Work experience

(b) • The names of your closest colleagues
   • What their jobs are
   • Who is the head of each department
   • The jobs you will have to do
   • How many hours you have to work
   Any two of the above

(c) • Once things are written down, you won't have to **try to remember them**
   • You will be able to **concentrate on other things**.

(d) Smile

(e) • Repeat their name out loud
   • It makes it easier to remember the name

(f) • Positive
   • Lively
   • Ready to take your projects forward
   Any one of the above

(g) This article is intended for: tick (✓) one box.

People who have been unemployed	
Young people facing their first job	✓
A new boss meeting staff for the first time	

Writing

Please see the assessment criteria for Writing on pages 148 to 150.

NATIONAL 5 SPANISH MODEL PAPER 3

Listening

Item 1

(a) • He does not live with them
  • Works in another town
  Any one of the above

(b) • Her father is a doctor
  • He **works long hours**

(c) Eat together as a family

(d) (i) Go to an Italian restaurant (near their house)
  (ii) • They are all relaxed
    • They talk and laugh
    Any of the above

(e) • Who is to wash the dishes
  • Who should take out the dog
  • When they should be home at night
  Any two of the above

(f) In your opinion, is Luisa positive about relationships in her family? Tick (✓) the correct box.

Not at all	
Very much so	
Overall, yes	✓

Item 2

(a) • 20 kilometres
  • South of Valencia
  • In a pretty area
  Any two of the above

(b) (i) It is noisy
  (ii) • There are a lot of people there
    • It is next to the church

(c) • When she is tired
  • When the weather is bad

(d) • Her **older** sister
  • On **Saturday** mornings

(e) Which of the following statements are correct? Tick (✓) two boxes.

My grandfather lives with us	
My mother is blonde with green eyes	
My sister is very serious	✓
I get on well with her	✓

(f) Near her house

(g) • They have the same tastes
  • Share the same interests.

NATIONAL 5 SPANISH 2014

Reading

1. (a) • Travelling/(desire/wanting) to travel
  • Living in another European country/other parts of Europe/live in Europe

  (b) (i) A big change in her life/a big change in her lifestyle/it changed her life greatly

    (ii) • (Discovered) a new city
      • (Discovered) a different city (to hers)
      • She visited places (around Brussels)/she visited the surroundings
      • She experienced/soaked up/absorbed another culture
      • She had a great/good time/it was good
    Any two of the above

  (c) • (Went home) knowing/learnt/could speak/talk English
    • (Another) education system
    • Be in contact with/got to know/got connected to/have/make relationships with other people
    Any two of the above

  (d) (i) • No day was the same (as the last)/every day was different/no 2 days were the same
      • There was/he **always** had something to do/there was lots to do
    (ii) • Way of seeing/his view of/how he saw the world

2. (a) • Acted/performed/actor in the theatre
  • He starred/acted in his first soap opera/at 11 he starred in a soap opera

  (b) (i) (It had a lot of) international success/hit

    (ii) • Political
      • Funny
      • (Very) emotional/exciting/moving
    Any two of the above

  (c) • Promoting/helping Oxfam's campaigns/Promoting Oxfam/Campaigning/campaigns for Oxfam
    • The (most) vulnerable (population/people)

  (d) • How difficult life was for the farmers/difficulties of being a farmer/difficult (time) to be a farmer/life was difficult for farmers
    • Farmers complain about the unfair trade/commercial system
    Any one of the above

  (e) • Went to meetings
    • Discussed ideas
    • Presented case studies
    • Talked to the Media
    • Handed in/out/over delivered petitions
    Any two of the above

3. (a) • Advertising/publicity/commercials
  • Business/commerce/industry
  • Communication/to communicate
  Any two of the above

  (b) • A good/better reputation
    • Business/commercial contacts/links

  (c) • Use/go on databases
    • Find information on the Internet/Web

(d) • Apps and programmes/used in applications and programmes

(e) • Deal with/face up to problems
• Start projects
• Solving (unforeseen/unexpected) difficulties/ Finding a solution to (unforeseen/unexpected) difficulties
• Get on with colleagues/workmates/be a team player
Any two of the above

(f) • It gives you advice on what skills you need in a job
Box 2

Writing

Please see the assessment criteria for Writing on pages 148 to 150.

NATIONAL 5 SPANISH 2014

Listening

Item 1

(a) • Basketball
• (He goes to the) gym.

(b) • (It contains) a lot of/too much grease/fat/it is very fatty/very greasy
• (It contains) too much/a lot of salt
Any one of the above

(c) • The vegetables are fresh
• The vegetables are good quality
Any one of the above

(d) fizzy drinks/fizzy juice

(e) • Liked/ate junk/fast food/rubbish
• His grandparents gave/made him cakes
• He (and his friends) bought sweets/caramels
Any two of the above

(f) He does lots to look after his health
(Box 1)

Item 2

(a) • Not much/not a lot
• (She goes to) the sports centre/leisure centre/sports hall
Any one of the above

(b) • Download songs
• Chat/talk to her friends
• Information for her homework/school work
Any two of the above

(c) She spends a lot of/too much time (using/on/the computer/online/on it)

(d) (i) (Many) people can see your profile
(ii) She keeps her profile/details/information private/to herself/hidden

(e) • Her friends live far away/doesn't live near her friends
• She can't/doesn't go out with/see/meet her friends much
Any one of the above

(f) • Reads about celebrities/searches famous people.
• Television/watches programmes
• Calendar
Any two of the above

(g) • Beach
• The shopping centre/mall/shops
• (Main/town/city) square

NATIONAL 5 SPANISH 2015

Reading

Text 1

(a) Want/wish/desire/need money
NB: Should have feeling of desire

(b) *Any one from:*
- Become/be independent
- Explore/see world of work/business
- Source of income

(c) • Go out to party/go out in the town/binge with friends
- Driving lessons/licence/test **or** to learn to drive

(d) *Any two from:*
- Stacking shelves in a supermarket
- Delivering papers/paper round
- Looking after/babysitting relatives' children

(e) *Any one from:*
- Teaches/helps her grandfather how to use the internet/go online
- Walks her neighbour's dogs

(f) (i) It's difficult to get up early/in the morning/ for school

(ii) *Any one from:*
- Go to school/class tired/sleepy/fall asleep in class
- Don't have time for/skip breakfast
- Learn hardly anything/learn nothing

(g) **MIDDLE BOX** — Having a part-time job while studying is difficult for many young people
NB: If more than one box is ticked, 0 marks are awarded.

Text 2

(a) Fifth/5

(b) • American sculptures
- Modern European art (in any order)

(c) They are going to love it/go crazy about it/go wild for it/be passionate about it/it will excite them

(d) • Less well-known/less famous artists
- Of the last 50 years/50 years old/from 50 years ago

(e) (i) Voting for/choosing their favourite work of art/ art/painting

(ii) • Touch/interactive/tactile screens
- Survey/questionnaire/evaluation online/on the webpage

(f) Free days/open days/free access for retired people/ pensioners/retired citizens/senior citizens

Text 3

(a) • Fast/quickly/at excess speed
- Carelessly/without care/not sensibly/not wisely
NB: Accept responses in any order

(b) (To improve) safety

(c) *Any two from:*
- Facial expressions
- Muscle movements
- Emotions on the face

(d) *Any two from:*
- If the driver is distracted/absent minded/not concentrating
- If the driver is sleepy/drowsy/tired
- If the driver is not in a condition to drive
NB: The driver only needs to be mentioned once

(e) • Sound/set off an alarm 5 times
- If s/he is sleeping/asleep

(f) *Any one from:*
- Avoids/prevents an accident
- Reduces risks (of human error)

Writing

Please see the assessment criteria for Writing on pages 148 to 150.

NATIONAL 5 SPANISH
2015

Listening

Item 1

(a) *Any one from:*
- Swiss/from Switzerland
- Speaks/knows/understands many/lots of languages
- Speaks French, Italian and German **(any 2 languages)**

(b) *Any one from:*
- She has an enthusiastic teacher
- (Learns/sings) songs
- Teacher has good sense of humour
NB: Ignore gender

(c) Interactive board/Smart board/active board/interactive screens/touch screens

(d) She helps/talks to/speaks to/communicates with tourists (visiting her town)

(e) Ireland
NB: Ignore wrong compass point

(f)
- Work for an international company/business/firm/office
- Travel/see/go around the world

(g) **BOTTOM BOX** — they play an important part in many areas of her life
NB: If more than one box is ticked, 0 marks are awarded.

Item 2

(a) Three hours
NB: Ignore additional information

(b)
- **BOX 2** — the first exam is Biology
- **BOX 4** — they last for 17 days in total
NB: If three boxes ticked, maximum 1 mark; if four boxes ticked, 0 marks are awarded.

(c) *Any two from:*
- It's not easy working alone
- Learns better/more
- Time passes quicker/quickly/fast/faster
- Not so bored/not boring

(d) *Any two from:*
- Eats biscuits
- Calls/phones/talks/speaks to/chats with friends
- Watches a soap opera/TV series/TV drama

(e) (Remembering/memorising/learning) the dates

(f) *Any two from:*
- Be/go/relax outdoors/outside/in the open air/out in fresh air
- Going out on his bike/cycling
- Training with his swimming club/swimming

(g) *Any two from:*
- It's on Wednesday
- He hasn't worked (enough)/he hasn't done enough
- He is not feeling well/feels ill/feels sick
- He has a sore throat

Acknowledgements

Permission has been sought from all relevant copyright holders and Hodder Gibson is grateful for the use of the following:

An article taken from www.studygs.net © Joe Landsberger (Model Paper 1 Writing page 3);
Image © jazzerup/Shutterstock.com (2014 Reading page 2);
Image © Featureflash/Shutterstock.com (2014 Reading page 4);
Image © Konstantin Chagin/Shutterstock.com (2014 Reading page 6);
Image © Stokkete/Shutterstock.com (2015 Reading page 2);
Image © zhu difeng/Shutterstock.com (2015 Reading page 4);
Image © Zurijeta/Shutterstock.com (2015 Reading page 6).

Hodder Gibson would like to thank SQA for use of any past exam questions that may have been used in model papers, whether amended or in original form.